D0289155

CHURCH
HISTORY

CHURCH HISTORY

A CRASH COURSE FOR THE CURIOUS

CHRISTOPHER CATHERWOOD

CROSSWAY BOOKS
WHEATON, ILLINOIS

Church History

Revised edition copyright © 2007 by Christopher Catherwood

Originally published as *Crash Course in Church History* in the United Kingdom by Hodder & Stoughton, copyright © 1998 by Christopher Catherwood.

Published by Crossway Books
          a publishing ministry of Good News Publishers
          1300 Crescent Street
          Wheaton, Illinois 60187

All rights reserved. No part of this publication may be reproduced, stored in a retrieval system or transmitted in any form by any means, electronic, mechanical, photocopy, recording or otherwise, without the prior permission of the publisher, except as provided for by USA copyright law.

Cover design: Jon McGrath

First printing, 2007

Printed in the United States of America

Scripture quotations are taken from *The Holy Bible: English Standard Version*®.
Copyright © 2001 by Crossway Bibles, a publishing ministry of Good News Publishers.
Used by permission. All rights reserved.

Library of Congress Cataloging-in-Publication Data
Catherwood, Christopher.
  Church history : a crash course for the curious / Christopher
Catherwood.—Rev. ed.
    p. cm.
  ISBN 13: 978-1-58134-841-5 (tpb)
  ISBN 10: 1-58134-841-X
  1. Church history. I. Title.
BR145.3.C365   2007
270—dc22   2006100050

VP		17	16	15	14	13	12	11	10	09	08	07
15	14	13	12	11	10	9	8	7	6	5	4	3	2

To my parents
Fred and Elizabeth Catherwood
who nourished my love of church history,
and to their wonderful daughter-in-law,
my wife Paulette
who has kept that love alive

Table of Contents

Acknowledgments

While most authors end their acknowledgments by thanking their patient spouse, here in Cambridge the fashion seems to be to begin that way. I think that this is an altogether more biblical approach since anyone fortunate enough to be married knows that no two people are as close as those whom God has joined together.

I therefore follow the Cambridge pattern and gratefully begin these acknowledgments with the profoundest of thanks, love, affection, and gratitude to my wife Paulette, the ideal helpmeet, companion, and soul mate whom God has provided me with these many years past. Paulette is the embodiment of the woman in Proverbs 31 and living proof that such women can and really do exist. She has been a constant muse and inspiration for everything that I write, and my gratitude to her can never be enough.

I am also profoundly thankful for editors. Having once been one myself, I know what hours of work they put in to make sure that what authors write is in a fit state to be published. Here I have been deeply blessed by having one of the most legendary, well-liked, and widely respected editors in Christian publishing, Allan Fisher, stand behind this book. He and I have known each other for many years now, and it is such a pleasure and privilege to be one of his authors at last. I was delighted to have Ted Griffin as the copy editor for this book.

All Crossway authors are also more than grateful to that splendid and godly couple Lane and Ebeth Dennis. I first stayed in their home over twenty years ago, and they have been a marvelous source of inspiration and encouragement ever since. Their ministry has transformed countless lives, and so too has the *English Standard Version,* much of which was translated just a few miles from where I am writing this. Thank God that Lane and Ebeth have kept the faith through their loyal service at Crossway Books.

These words have been written in the attic in the fifteenth-century part of my parents' home, a lovely old house a few miles outside of Cambridge, England. I am most grateful to them for providing this facility when my eighteenth-century office in Cambridge itself fell through. But they also deserve the dedication, along with my wife, of this book, since both of them have nurtured my interest in Christian history, and in history in general, ever since I was young (and my mother's father, the late Dr. D. Martyn Lloyd-Jones, in his lifetime as well). My thanks to them, too, cannot ever be enough.

This is the first book that I have written since that wonderful church historian, the Rev. John S. Moore, died in early 2006. Thankfully he knew the contract would be signed just before he passed away. He spent over three decades editing a church history magazine, and his library was comparable in scope to that of my grandfather, Dr. Lloyd-Jones, whom he will now have met at last in heaven. John Moore was a great example of how to write accurate church history, and he passed all of his skills in precision and accuracy on to his daughter, my wife Paulette.

I have been so fortunate in the institutions with which I have been affiliated these past years. The first, most important of all for a church historian, is my own church, St Andrew the Great in Cambridge. This has many historical links in itself, not least with the great Cambridge Puritan Richard Sibbes, who was closely associated with it in days past. Thankfully the current staff has maintained that Puritan devotion to godly life and preaching, and my thanks to the current incumbent, the

Rev. Mark Ashton, and his team over the past sixteen years are considerable. For most of our time there Paulette and I have been small group
Bible study leaders and have been consistently encouraged and blessed
by those in our group. Members while I wrote this book included Mark
Cardwell, Derek Wright, and Richard and Sally Reynolds, and their
prayerful support of my writing has been wonderful.

St Edmund's College Cambridge has been my academic base in
Cambridge since 1994, and I have been associated with it in various
roles since then. Here again numerous people have been encouragement itself, including, among many others, the former Master, Sir
Brian Heap, who is as enthusiastic a fellow evangelical as he is eminent
as a scientist; Dr. Brian Stanley, the distinguished missiologist and
Baptist historian; the vice-master Dr. Geoffrey Cook; the treasurer Dr.
Simon Mitton; the bursar Mrs. Moira Gardiner; and the numerous
members of the Senior Common Room, permanent and visiting (usually from literally all over the world) who make my lunchtime visits
always so intellectually stimulating and personally enjoyable.

I also teach church history, among other subjects, for the Institute
of Economic and Political Studies (INSTEP) here in Cambridge. This
is a Junior Year Abroad program—not part of the university but linked
to many well-known American universities and colleges, including
Tulane, Wake Forest, Villanova, Trinity College in Connecticut, and
several similar places. Here my warmest thanks go to that highly well-
regarded and quintessentially Cambridge couple Professor Geoffrey
Williams and his wife Janice, who direct the Institute, for giving me
pupils to keep body and soul together. This is especially the case when
those students choose to subsidize my writing by wanting to study
something about which I am also writing a book.

I had the privilege of receiving a doctorate from the University of
East Anglia while writing this book, and my gratitude to my legendary
supervisor, Professor John Charmley, is correspondingly profound.

I also have the enormous annual pleasure of teaching and writing
at the University of Richmond in Richmond, Virginia. I have been an
annual teacher at the Summer School of their School of Continuing

Studies for many years now and also, equally helpfully, the Annual Writer in Residence for the university's History Department. Everyone in both departments has been consistently wonderful to their annual visiting Briton, and I am deeply grateful to all of the people involved both there and in the International Program. The Boatwright Library has also been a superb place in which to do research since its resources are much more generous than those of most university libraries. John and Susan Gordon, Fred and Nancy Anderson, John Treadway and Marina Scheidt, Pat and Dewey Johnson, David Kitchen and Michele Cox, Hugh West, Bob Kenzer, Cheryl Genovese, Jim Narduzzi, Douglass Young, Roger Brooks, Victoria Halman, Krittika Onsanit, Jane Dowrick, and countless other people, from the Heilman Center to the Boatwright, have been American hospitality personified. I am most grateful to all of them.

My in-laws have been great during my visits to the USA. Let me give warmest thanks and gratitude to all the splendid members of the Moore and Paulette families for many years of kindness, down to little Tyler Crabbe, my first great-nephew, who was born in 2005 on his great-grandfather John Moore's last and eighty-seventh birthday. I thank them most warmly for their effortless hospitality and love over numerous visits.

My in-laws have been consistently supportive of all my writing and kindly tolerant of a non-Virginian interloper in their midst. The Moores and Paulettes are too numerous to mention individually. But I can say that knowing them has been a joy and pleasure these many years of married life, and I am profoundly grateful to each and every one of them, and to those fellow in-laws who share the joy of marrying into so splendid a set of families. You know who you are and how thankful I am to all of you, not least in providing the most ideal wife possible in Paulette.

Many thanks go too to some wonderful Christian friends in Virginia: Lamar and Betsy Brandt (and her mother Bettie Woodson Weaver), Claude and Leigh Marshall, and Larry and Beth Adams. Equal gratitude goes to those at Second Baptist Church of Richmond, the Moore family church, who have been so kind to me and to my wife and in-laws since I first appeared in their church back in 1991. As with my in-laws, they are too numerous to mention, but they know who they are.

This is the new and completely revised edition of a book first published in the United Kingdom in 1998 by Hodder & Stoughton. Many thanks go to all those involved in that first edition. I also taught a course for Cambridge University's Institute of Continuing Education based upon that book, and warm thanks go to Graham Howes and Linda Fisher who made those lectures possible and to those who attended the course itself in Cambridge.

Finally, thanks to all of you on my e-mail prayer list—here again, there are far too many to mention individually—who have consistently prayed for me and my writing over many years. Your prayerful support and encouragement, often from thousands of miles away, show what a wonderful thing both prayer and Christian fellowship really are.

Christopher Catherwood
Cambridge, England
Richmond, Virginia
2006

Introduction

As evangelical Christians we are people who believe in the historicity of a book, the Bible. This is, as Francis Schaeffer reminded us back at Lausanne in 1974, one of our distinctive features as evangelicals, something that separates us from other professing Christians.

But for how many of us does our knowledge of the history of God's people end where the New Testament finishes, in the first century? Perhaps we remember hearing about the Reformation and recall that things of which we approve happened, but even there we forget most of the details; even there our memories are often hazy. But events took place then that five hundred years later still define us as evangelical Christians. We remain children of the Reformation even today.

Sometimes we know a bit about the history of our own denomination or of heroic figures of the past such as John Knox, Thomas Cranmer, John Wesley, George Whitefield, or John Smyth and Thomas Helwys, Jan Hus, Martin Luther, John Calvin, Huldreich Zwingli, and Menno Simons, depending upon the part of the church from which we come. But even there our memory is often shaky, and with so many evangelicals now attending independent churches, with no denominational affiliation, only just a few years old in many cases, that historic denominational memory no longer applies.

Yet cutting ourselves off from the past is a very dangerous thing to do.

We know that Christians alive today are our brothers and sisters in Christ. But so too are those fellow true believers who lived in the two thousand years of church history before us. We are all God's children, regardless of the century in which we lived or live. They loved the same Savior, read (especially after the Reformation) the same Bible, and shared all the spiritual ups and downs through which we go today. Technology may have changed, but God's truth and the human condition never change, and we see that clearly through the unfolding patterns of Christian history.

Why do we do many of the things we take for granted? Why is Scripture so central to the lives of God's people? It is easy today to go into a bookstore and pick up the *English Standard Version* (or the *Evangelically Sound Version* as some people call it). But in the past our fellow Christians were prepared to sacrifice their own lives, often in barbaric ways, such as being burned alive at the stake, simply so ordinary people could read the Bible in a language they could understand.

Prior to 1989 and the fall of the Iron Curtain I used to spend quite a large amount of time with Christians living on the Communist, totalitarian side of that barrier. We always had the impression that anyone who survived persecution must be some kind of extra-holy super-Christian. But in fact most of them were just like us, which made their Christian faith in often appalling circumstances all the more amazing, because they survived such terrible times *without* being special or exceptionally holy.

It is the same with the Christians who lived before us.

One of the things that shows that the Bible is truly God's Word is that it does not hide human frailty—God alone is righteous. Peter denied Jesus out of fright and confessed he found Paul's epistles a little hard to understand sometimes. Paul and Barnabas fell out and parted company. We can all identify with the very human people we read about in Scripture. Yet look at what amazing things they did! It is the same throughout history—God uses often remarkably ordinary individuals to achieve extraordinary things.

Most modern heresies, for example, are not new but are recycled versions of errors long past, simply presenting themselves in updated guise. If we know our church history, we can compare present to past and arm ourselves against false teaching accordingly.

In the twenty-first century we are always trying to reinvent the wheel and behave accordingly, as if nobody has ever tried to do what we are now attempting to achieve. History shows that this is almost never the case. The mechanism might change—we could not fly before 1900, for example—but the principles remain exactly the same. We can now cross the Atlantic in a matter of hours, not weeks. But human nature is no different in the twenty-first century than it was in the first.

Put first-century Jews or Romans in jeans and sweatshirts and place them on a subway in a twenty-first-century modern city and you would not notice the difference. Read, for example, the letters home from soldiers from Italy or North Africa, garrisoned at the Roman frontier fortress of Vindolanda on Hadrian's Wall in freezing northern Britain, and you could be reading letters home from American troops in Iraq today.

In other words, Henry Ford was wrong. History is *not* bunk. It is our connection to our fellow human beings who just happened to live in the centuries before us.

When we read the Bible, especially the historical narratives, from Genesis through Acts, we also see that there is a learning or didactic purpose to history. Again, God's Word does not hide the frailties of His people—for example, Abraham pretending that Sarah is his sister or Thomas having doubts. Yet God accomplished great things through such people.

It is my purpose to be equally didactic, to write a history from which we can all learn something of what God has done through His church over the centuries.

However, as is obvious, there is one rather large difference. I am not writing an infallible, inerrant book of Holy Scripture. As we shall see,

Christians have differed with each other over the past two thousand years, and often strongly. One of the great tragedies is that even believing Christians have persecuted each other, with one set of Protestants, for example, putting to death another for disagreements over issues such as baptism.

If one takes baptism as an example of divergences, consider your reaction to the statement, usually made as a joke, "You baptize people your way, and I'll do it God's way." I have heard that joke made by both Baptists and Presbyterians, whose theology of baptism is not at all the same.

Obviously as a theologically conservative Calvinist Baptist attending an equally theologically conservative Anglican church (that is also Reformed theologically and prefers to baptize people by believer's baptism by immersion despite being in the Church of England), I have biases of my own!

In Scripture we get God's eye view since the authors were writing as inspired by the Holy Spirit. No other authors can claim such inspiration. Were the Christians of the fourth century right to come to an accommodation with the emperor, for example, to take one issue over which genuine Christians have disagreed with each other for hundreds of years? Was the Swiss Reformer Zwingli right to go into battle? The history of such events all take place after the unique revelation of Scripture came to an end, and I trust that we would agree, as evangelicals, whatever our denomination, that God does not reveal to us new things not contained in the Bible. Obviously, therefore, writing a book on church history is not as easy as it looks.

In Britain because evangelicals are, alas, comparatively few in number, we tend to collaborate across denominational lines. I have also been active for my entire adult life in interdenominational evangelical student ministry, especially the International Fellowship of Evangelical Students (IFES). On my side of the Atlantic, being Reformed and Baptist at the same time (let alone Episcopalian) is not unusual. While in the USA folk such as Mark Dever on the East Coast and John MacArthur on the West Coast (to take two highly regarded Crossway authors) also manage to combine the two, I know that others might regard this as somewhat unusual.

So being a mix of Reformed (on the doctrines of grace) and Baptist (on the issue of baptism) and attending an evangelical church that is both and coincidentally Anglican is fine with me. I hope this means that what follows is free of denominational bias, and I am certainly keen to be as objective as possible.

But being very happily married to an American evangelical of like persuasion, I do know that on her side of the Pond denominational loyalties can be stronger. In addition, as denominations tend to be far larger there, it is not always the case that an evangelical of one denomination meets those from another.

However, Dr. D. Martyn Lloyd-Jones, that great twentieth-century preacher (and posthumous Crossway author) always said of himself that he was a "Bible Calvinist," not a "System Calvinist." This has always been my own motto, and as we shall see when we study the Reformation, it is at the heart of the key Protestant distinctive, *sola scriptura*, or "Scripture alone."

As evangelicals we are Bible Christians, believers not in tradition but centered around what we believe God's Word to us is teaching. Otherwise we are not really any different from the Catholic Church, from which our Protestant forebears split. That Church taught—and still teaches—that the tradition of the Church is equal in authority to that of the Bible. If we put our denominational tradition first, we are being no different, and the Reformation was for nothing. So while for some people being a Reformed Baptist might seem a little strange, for others it is simply following what the Bible teaches.

But I do think, if one looks at the ways in which Christians have put together statements of faith over the centuries, that there *are* key things upon which all Bible-believing Christians do and have always agreed and united.

That does not mean we believe the same on everything, including issues such as baptism, church government, the continuation of the gift of tongues, or whatever other issues divide us. But as Christocentric

Bible believers there are certain core truths, such as the atonement, resurrection, and evangelism, upon which all of us as evangelicals do believe exactly the same thing. It is from that perspective, and how those beliefs unfold through history, that this book will be written.

So what follows will be from a strongly evangelical perspective, written from the theological point of view that what God says to us in His Word is what Francis Schaeffer so aptly called "true truth." This book is unashamedly cross-centered and takes the Bible to be authentically true.

But it will also not avoid areas in which honest Christians have lovingly—and, alas, in times past not so lovingly—disagreed with one another. This can be a minefield if we let where we differ predominate over where we agree. I can understand this. But being, for example, on Zwingli's side on the issue of Communion but equally on the side, regarding baptism, of those Anabaptists he had put to death for heresy, I can understand both conflicting points of view simultaneously.

A penultimate point for those who might have seen the earlier edition of this book, published in the United Kingdom in 1998 and just distributed in the USA: that book was designed for what might be called the crossover market, for sales as much in secular bookstores as in Christian. In that edition I had to tread slightly warily of too overtly a partisan perspective, and it was necessary to be as neutral as possible. In this new Crossway edition I still aim to be denominationally neutral, even though I have revealed my own inclinations in this Introduction since many readers would naturally want to know the theological perspective from which I am coming. But as I imagine that most readers will share my evangelical interpretation, a standpoint that is taken by Scripture-believing Christians in many different denominations and independent churches alike, I should say that in this edition those firm evangelical views will be apparent throughout.

One final important theological point needs to be made. As Christians we believe not only that God acts through history and through ordinary people but also that there is such a thing as absolute truth out there. Schaeffer's "true truth" is not a tautology.

In today's postmodern world this is not something fashionable to say. Every group has its own "narratives," none of which might be "privileged" over the other one—unless, of course, you come from a favored group such as Marxists, feminists, a fashionable minority, or whatever is deemed acceptable by those who decide such things.

For science graduates reading this, as D. A. Carson pointed out in a lecture he gave, all this might seem meaningless. Scientists need absolutes to be able to conduct experiments and carry out most of their working lives. This is far from the case in the humanities, however. To be a Marxist historian might be all right—Marxists do believe in absolutes, albeit the wrong ones, but Marxism is an acceptable "narrative." But writing history that still holds to absolute truth, and especially one that believes that Christianity is completely true, is to be most unfashionable.

Sadly, even some Christian historians I know feel that no one should know they are Christians through what they write. In some areas declarations of faith may not be needed. In my history of how Churchill created Iraq in 1921, for example, Christianity per se does not enter into the story. But on a subject like this one, the story of the Christian church, it is obviously impossible to keep out my own perspectives, and that very much includes a belief in absolute truth.

Thankfully not all universities are plagued with postmodern mush. Here in Cambridge, the Regius (= main; literally "Crown Appointed") Professor of History, an expert on the Third Reich, has published *In Defence of History*. Richard Evans makes the telling point that if all "narratives" have equal validity, then so does the Nazi. On their own criteria, the postmodernists have no grounds for saying that the Jewish belief in the absolute moral horror of the Holocaust is preferable as a "narrative" over and above the Nazis who say that to exterminate six million Jews—not to mention twenty million Russians, Gypsies, Lutheran pastors, and others—is perfectly all right.

As a Christian I have no problem at all in saying that genocide is evil! The past is not a series of competing "narratives" or "stories," all of which are equally valid. There are rights and wrongs, and all Christians should and can see God working providentially throughout history.

To me, people who claim to write "objective" history— that is, history without bias—are almost invariably people who, when writing on religious history, have a strong bias against evangelical belief, the existence of the supernatural, or the guiding hand of God in providence. Our political prejudices are man-made, however strongly we believe in them, and I am always careful to try to weed out such opinions from my analysis of the past. Christianity is God-made, not human, while, say, a Baptist or Methodist bias might be unfair regarding other equally good Christian perspectives. But a strong belief in the truth of the atonement, of God's very existence, and of a meaning to history because God is in charge of it is surely to adopt a biblical rather than human interpretation of what happens and why. As Christians living in postmodern times, we ought to reclaim the idea that there is a final truth that God has revealed through Jesus Christ on the cross and that we live in a universe of which God is in control, and therefore it has meaning.

On that note, let us now proceed with the story.

From Christ to Constantine

C hristianity is a faith named after its founder. We are above all as Christians believers in a person—Jesus Christ. Muslims get angry when they are called Mohammedans since the name of their faith is Islam, which means "submission" in Arabic. Muhammad (or Mohammed) may be that religion's founder, but he was emphatic in saying that he was not divine. Hinduism is the religion of an ethnic group—the Indians of South Asia. Judaism is also today an ethnic faith, although in times past proselytes, outsiders like Naaman the Syrian, occasionally joined.

Christianity is unique, worshiping a divine founder as God, God the Son, Jesus Christ. We are saved not by good works, as is the norm in man-made faiths, but through the fully accomplished salvation we have in Jesus Christ through His atonement on the cross. Ours is a very *personal* faith.

So the beginning of Christianity is centered around an individual, Jesus of Nazareth, who we Christians know is God incarnate, come down to live among sinners like us to reconcile us with God.

23

While there are many precepts, moral codes, teachings, and so on in Christianity, our faith is above all a redeemed relationship. Not only that, but it is God coming down to us rather than humans trying to reach up to God.

As Paul reminds us, if Christ is not risen, our hope is in vain. Ours is also a historic religion, and here it again differs from others, which evolved over the course of time, such as the varying branches of Buddhism and Hinduism. We believe in both a person and in facts connected to that person, things that really happened in what Francis Schaeffer liked to call space and time.

Not only that, but the church itself consists of people. We are not simply an institution, but countless individuals all uniquely related to each other through the special individual relationship we each have with God through Christ. Do remember, when looking at church history, that in Scripture the church is seen as a person, the Bride of Christ, and not as an institution. That is not to deny institutional aspects of God's church here on earth. But what we are looking at is the unfolding story of people and what happened to them throughout history.

Christianity also arose in the context of a specific historical background, the multinational, multiethnic, and multireligious Roman Empire. To us as Christians this ought to be no coincidence—it was all planned that way by God Himself. The events that led to the large-scale Roman Empire, which stretched from the Atlantic coast of Spain in the west to the borders of present-day Iraq in the east, all having their origins hundreds of years before Christ came to earth, God planned centuries in advance.

Providential History

Are things in our own lives (the small scale) or in history (the large scale) ever purely random events? To use Einstein's famous phrase in another context, does God play dice? Surely for us as Christians, with a knowledge through the Bible of how God acts, the answer to that must be no. God not only knows what is going to happen but also arranges things so that His will takes place.

On an individual level this is a profoundly comforting doctrine. However odd things may sometimes seem to us, we can have complete faith that our lives are not arbitrary and that God knows what He is doing and is seeking to accomplish.

But while many Christians gain comfort from this at the micro-level, we all too often forget that this is true of the big picture as well, of history itself.

I call this *providential history* because *all* that happens, whether simply to us as individuals or on the global scale, to rulers and nations, is equally in the all-loving, omniscient hands of God.

We see this clearly laid out in Scripture because the narrator tells us that God hardened Pharaoh's heart and put it into the mind of Cyrus to let the children of Israel return home. But as we shall see throughout this book, it is evident that God continues to arrange historical events, so that His purposes can be worked out.

So I do not think it presumptuous to say that this is the case for the historical and cultural circumstances into which Christ came and in which early Christianity was able to grow so rapidly over such an enormous geographical area.

The first of these providential circumstances is probably one we know from childhood Bible stories. The Roman Empire is the background to the New Testament. We are aware that God had predicted it many centuries earlier in the visions He gave to Daniel, when Rome was no more than a blip on a very distant horizon, a small and insignificant city-state in a peninsula with little world importance. By Christ's time it ruled a vast empire from Spain to Iraq, including therefore not only Palestine but also all the other regions around the Mediterranean.

This meant political stability, which enormously helped the spread of the gospel since it was not necessary to cross over unfriendly borders to bring the message to a wide region. It was possible, for example, to go from the Scottish border in northern Europe to the frontiers of

Sudan in Africa in the south, all within the safe confines of Roman rule. Never before had one such gigantic political unit existed, and after Christianity had spread throughout it, the Roman Empire split, never again to be reunited on such a scale.

But since the Romans were some of the best road builders the world has ever seen, it also meant that the logistics of travel became much easier. Roman roads were immensely efficient and, thanks to firm political control, also safe.

The other massive help was linguistic/cultural. This is not so evident to us now when reading the Bible. But it is to those who read it in its original language—Greek, or in particular, *koine* or popular Greek.

Here we can say that God had paved the way over three hundred years earlier through the megalomania of the great Macedonian—and Greek-speaking—conqueror Alexander the Great. He created within a few years an enormous empire stretching from Greece in the west, Egypt in the south, and Bactria in present-day Afghanistan, on the borders of the Hindu Kush in the east. (During the 2001 invasion of Afghanistan we probably all read articles about fair-haired Afghans, descendants over two millennia later of the original invading Greek armies.)

The actual empire did not survive Alexander. But the successor states, including those that ruled over Egypt (the Ptolemies, including Cleopatra) and Iran (the Seleucids), remained culturally and linguistically Greek for centuries—look at the references in the New Testament to Greek speakers and Greek cities such as the Decapolis. In Egypt a large Greek population remained down to the twentieth century. In fact the Egyptian city Alexandria was named directly after Alexander himself.

This meant that from Greece to the Indian border there were people who either were Greeks, thought along Greek lines (the Hellenizers of the New Testament), or spoke Greek as a second language. Already, long before Christ, the Old Testament had been translated into Greek—the Septuagint. So when Christ came, the simplest and most widespread common language into which to write the good news, our New Testament, was therefore Greek, not Latin. And all this was because of the mania for conquest of a pagan ruler living three hundred years before the birth of Christ.

This, therefore, is the political and cultural background to the extraordinarily rapid and wide spread of the Christian message in the first century. It reached from Spain in the west to Syria in the east, Macedonia in the north and Ethiopia in the south, all by the end of the book of Acts.

To secular historians, all this is helpful coincidence, as will be the case with many other events in Christian history, such as the Reformation, as we will see. But I do not think we can see it like that. Surely these two extraordinary conjunctions—the size and stability of the Roman Empire and the multinational and equally geographically large use of Greek as a second language—cannot just be accidents. So helpful were they to the easy spreading of the gospel and making Christianity a global faith so early on that they must be seen as part of the providence of God.

As Edith Schaeffer reminds us in her book *Christianity Is Jewish*, the Jewish background to the origins of Christianity is vital to remember. Jesus Himself was Jewish, as were all His early disciples. Much of the book of Acts is taken up with Jewish-related themes, with Peter realizing that the Old Testament dietary laws no longer applied, and Paul using Jewish synagogues as jumping-off points in his early missionary journeys.

In the entire ancient world the Jews were unique. As I show in my secular history book *A Brief History of the Middle East*, they alone were monotheists. Nowadays, with the two major global monotheistic faiths—Islam and Christianity—being both monotheistic and multicultural, we forget how extraordinarily unusual this was in ancient times. *All* the other major religions were polytheistic, believing in vast pantheons of gods and goddesses, as Hinduism does today, or in numerous manifestations of deity, as is the case with Buddhism. Even if your own religion had few gods, people believed that gods related to a particular ethnic group—Jupiter and Neptune for the Romans, for example—and that no one group's deities were unique. It was the Jews, and the Jews alone, who believed that not merely was their God the God of Israel, but *that no other gods existed at all.* Furthermore, God related to His people and could be known. Nor was He capricious, like so many of the pagan deities, but profoundly moral. The Jews therefore, to use the phrase of a British writer, Paul Johnson, believed in *ethical monotheism.*

The Roman emperors basically could not care less what local deities their subject peoples worshiped, since the idea of exclusivity in religion was entirely alien to pagan peoples. However, they did insist on what one might call political religion—you could worship whomsoever you wished so long as you recognized the Roman emperor as being divine. This was essentially not a religious requirement but a political one, a way of ensuring that the vast Roman domains had the glue of common worship of the head of the Empire, the emperor.

Just one group was exempt from this—the Jews. Only they were permitted to worship their own God and no other, and they were not obliged to make religious sacrifices to the emperor.

By the first century Jews were spread all over the Empire and beyond. They could be found in the Persian Empire and as far afield as India. Wherever the Jews went, there were also synagogues where the faithful gathered. These were the Jews of the *Diaspora*, the beginnings of the spread of the Jewish people all over the world, in our own time in the United States and western Europe as well.

Since the earliest leaders of the infant Christian faith were also Jewish, it was only natural that they would begin by visiting the synagogues to proclaim Jesus as the true Jewish Messiah that He was. But as we see in the book of Acts other Jews rejected the claim, and the early church was persecuted.

Here, as I show in *Divided by God*, there is already a critical difference between the origin of Christianity and that of Islam, the other major transnational faith. As we shall see in the relevant chapter, Islam began as a religion of political and military power. Islam has always been linked to a state, preferably one under its own rule, the Realm or

Dar al-Islam. Christianity, the Jewish writer Bernard Lewis has shown in his many books, is entirely different. For its first three centuries the Christians were viciously persecuted. This was done first by those Jews who rejected the messiahship of Jesus and, secondly, when the Romans, observing this, realized that Judaism and Christianity were actually two quite separate religions.

This Roman realization is important because in discovering the difference between the two faiths, the Romans decided that Christians were not protected by the Jewish exemption to worship the Roman emperor as divine. Christians, from early on, were subject to the full rigors of the Roman state and, refusing to worship Caesar as god, were persecuted most savagely for the next three centuries.

Persecution

Christians have been persecuted from the very beginning. One only has to read the book of Acts, several epistles—which reveal the fact that Paul was writing them from jail—and advice on how to deal with persecution in Peter's writing to see that being a Christian and being persecuted for that fact often went together in those days.

In other words, if Christians are being persecuted now, which they still are in many parts of the world, this is nothing at all new.

In fact Jesus Himself told His disciples to expect it, and throughout the history of the church in many parts of the world it has been the norm rather than the exception.

However, this has usually *increased* the church rather than diminished it, thereby doing the exact opposite of what the persecutors wanted to happen. As early church historian Tertullian declared, "The blood of the martyrs is the seed of the church." Throughout the period examined in this chapter, Christianity was an illegal, oppressed religion, and countless brave early Christians were put to death, often in vicious circumstances such as being burned alive or eaten alive. Yet the church grew rather than becoming extinct.

We see this again and again throughout history. In the late twentieth century a terrible wave of persecution hit the churches in China, and numerous Christians were sent off to barbaric prison camps, with many losing their lives. As one survivor told me in Beijing, the Christians during that time had a wonderful sense of the presence of God with them, sustaining them throughout the horror.

As with the persecution by the Romans, the campaign against Christianity had the exact opposite effect of that intended by the Chinese authorities. Christianity numbered around two million adherents, many of them very nominal, when the Communists took power in 1949. In the early twenty-first century and several waves of persecution later, there are at least seventy million Christians in China, if not far more. Not only has persecution winnowed out nominal believers, but the witness of enduring faith against such opposition has acted as a major source of evangelism—millions of Chinese have been profoundly impressed by how Christians have behaved in such atrocious circumstances. Martyrdom remains the seed of the church.

When Christians Disagree

In the Introduction to this book we ruled out the possibility of chance, and it is probably no coincidence that on the day I am writing this section, my Bible reading in the *English Standard Version* is 1 Corinthians 1. Even at the very dawn of the church itself, Christians were disagreeing with one another, and we have been doing so vigorously ever since.

Sometimes we are tempted to look back nostalgically to the dawn of our faith and think how wonderful it must have been to be united, unlike Christians now. But a swift canter through the epistles soon shows that such a view would be mistaken.

Obviously, as Paul demonstrates in his letters, some disagreement is entirely sinful, having more to do with pride and jostling for power and position than anything else. Sometimes personality clashes are involved, as the apostle implies at the end of his epistle to the Philippians. But with others, genuine doctrinal divergence is apparent, and this became increasingly the case after the original disciples died and the New Testament was completed (more on this issue later). Even in Paul's lifetime there were genuine differences among believing Christians over the continued role of Jewish ritual observance, as we see in his debates with James in Jerusalem.

Now we have Presbyterians, Baptists, Methodists, Episcopalians, Pentecostals, and numerous other divisions. But at the same time, in Britain, the USA, and elsewhere evangelical Christians are often coming together in gospel unity despite doctrinal differences on issues such as church structure, baptism, spiritual gifts, and the like. We can unite around our regard for Scripture and on core doctrines such as the atonement.

As evangelicals we are, rightly I think, wary of ecumenism, of what one might call lowest-common-denominator unity, based as often as not on pretending we do not have real differences, especially for those for whom doctrine is not really very important. But we evangelicals often find that we have what we might describe as highest-common-factor unity in the gospel and in the core doctrines of Christian faith upon which all God's redeemed children inevitably agree with one another. So perhaps we are not as disunited as we think. I find that an encouraging thought.

From Montanus to Azusa Street?

The Montanists were an early Christian group who believed in hearing directly from God. They also spoke in tongues. So were they the forerunners of today's charismatics and Pentecostals?

I mention this because they are a classic example of the way in which Christians today can read contemporary disputes in the present back into the past and reinterpret the past not in its own light but in that of disagreements that we have today.

Non-Christians do such things all the time, including the appropriation of historical Christian figures for secular purposes. For example, the pre-1989 Communist government of Czechoslovakia, which was atheistic and anti-Christian, used Jan Hus, the great fifteenth-century reformer, as a national hero even though they would persecute people who shared his views in the twentieth century. They saw Hus as an anti-imperialist figure who stood up to the emperor of his day, and they thus saw him as a martyr to the cause of national freedom and revolution. Needless to say, this use of Hus, especially when combined with the persecution of his later followers, is entirely inappropriate. But it is another classic example of misusing the past to suit present-day needs.

The Montanists believed, as do mainline charismatics and Pentecostals today, that the miraculous sign gifts continued beyond the time of the apostles and continued to be available to ordinary Christians.

But that is where I would argue that direct comparisons end. The "prophecies" made by Montanus himself and by some of his key followers, such as Prisca and Montilla, did not come to pass. In addition, while the major church leader Tertullian joined them, no other people of his stature became Montanists, and by the fifth century the group had effectively died out.

Because the prophecies remained unfulfilled, and because the Montanists themselves did not survive, many today would argue that they were a detour away from mainstream doctrine, even though it is clear that their doctrines on key issues such as the atonement were entirely orthodox. They were Christians but essentially misguided.

Does that mean that Pentecostals and charismatic Christians today are equally misled? Is it fair to say that because the prophecies proved false, or were simply misguided, all such phenomena today are equally mistaken or even heretical?

The sign gifts are one of those issues upon which sincere evangelicals disagree with each other today. I bring up the Montanists in order to raise the important theological issue of *why* we as evangelicals believe what we do. In that sense our own view, in this case regarding prophecy and speaking in tongues, is irrelevant. What matters above all is the source of our doctrine, and secondarily, in this context, our use of the past.

As evangelicals we are often glad to be described, even if it is by hostile outsiders, as "Bible-believing Christians." We will see in the Reformation chapter the critical importance doctrinally of the principle of *sola scriptura*, "by Scripture alone." We determine our doctrine by what the Bible says and not by the tradition of the church, one of the two key areas upon which Luther split from the Roman Catholic Church.

However, if we see something in the past that seems to vindicate something we do in the present, we all too easily leap upon it and use it to justify contemporary practice. So if we do believe in the sign gifts, the fact that a major early Christian grouping did so as well means that we are not alone in our particular doctrinal slant and that we are vindicated by what some Christians did in the past.

Similarly, if we are cessationist in our view of such matters, we grasp the fact that the prophecies were unfulfilled and that most Christians rejected Montanism as a rationale for our rejection of such theology in the twenty-first century.

One of the key messages of this book is that history *does* matter! I am not denying that for one moment.

On the other hand, it is vital for us as evangelicals that having rejected the tradition of the church as an equal source of contemporary authority, we do not then invent traditions of our own and make them as important as Scripture itself. Plenty of people do precisely this, but they cannot really call themselves evangelical if they do.

So, to take the Montanist issues of tongues and prophecy, are they valid for Christians today?

Well, surely the evangelical approach is to examine what Scripture says and to take our response from that rather than basing our beliefs on whether we think a group of second-century Christians, the Montanists, were right or not. We may not end up agreeing with one another—this is an issue over which evangelicals have disagreed, often strongly, since the reappearance of Pentecostalism in the twentieth century. But at least we will have decided on biblical grounds and not on tradition.

"I'll Baptize Them God's Way"

How did believers baptize people in early times?

If we knew beyond doubt the answer to that thorny question, there would not today be Baptists and Presbyterians, or at least not in the form that we know them today. (Many denominations now practice believer's baptism by immersion, and Baptists are therefore no longer unique in their methodology.)

The simple but inconvenient fact is that though we *do* know much about the practice of the early church, there is also much that is mysterious to us because the archaeological evidence is not as conclusive as we would like, regardless of which view we take. If sincere evangelicals can interpret the Bible in different ways on baptism, so too can archaeology. What has been discovered can be interpreted in different ways. What does it mean, for example, when we read that "households" were baptized? Were all the people in that household equally converted? We hope so, but firmer evidence is needed to be able to pronounce definitively.

But there are things, thankfully, upon which we can all agree. Baptism was clearly something commanded in the early church—"repent and be baptized" (Acts 2:38). So however it happens, it is not some nice optional extra. While we differ on this issue today, there does not seem to have been division over it back then. Perhaps this is a lesson for us today—to unite on the things that do matter, such as salvation, and to proclaim the message of repentance even if we differ on the methodology of what happens next.

How Do We Know What We Know?

How do we know what we know about so much of what happened in the early Christian centuries?

Much is from surviving manuscripts and letters. Because of the importance of the Scriptures, God's written Word to us, Christians have always been good at keeping manuscripts, and these include the writings of early Christian leaders as well as the actual Scriptures themselves.

Inevitably this means that we know more about the lives of famous Christian leaders than we do about ordinary, run-of-the-mill Christians who made up their congregations. That, though, has always been the case, in this as well as in other historical areas, although in more recent times historians have been busy trying to plug the gaps.

Can the New Testament Be Trusted?

The answer to this question is yes, and that is very important for the credibility of the Christian gospel in the skeptical age in which we live.

Do people believe in Caesar's *Gallic Wars*, the story of how Julius Caesar conquered what is now France? The answer is overwhelmingly yes, despite the fact that the earliest extant manuscripts that we have date from nine hundred years *after* Caesar wrote them—there are no contemporary copies. Nor are there many manuscripts at all.

With the Bible, especially the New Testament, it is radically different. We have thousands of manuscripts from as far back as the end of the first century and the beginning of the second. This is *decades* after the originals were written, not centuries as is the case with many of the documents historians and archaeologists believe were first composed in ancient times.

So before we go on to look at the issue in technical detail, why the complete acceptance of Caesar as the true author of his accounts of conquest but scholarly scorn toward the considerably better authenticated history of the New Testament documents?

As evangelicals, I think we are able to say that the real difference is not one of scholarship but is spiritual. If the New Testament documents are authentic, then they require a spiritual response to the Person about whom they are written, a response to the claims of Jesus Christ upon all our lives. If the documents are true, then the Christian case has to be taken seriously, and that is something that non-Christians, particularly theological liberals who reject Christ's supernatural nature, do not want to do. They reject the Scriptures not so much on an academic level but on a personal one. Of course, they dress up their rejection in scholarly language, sadly often with much condescension. By the way, in my experience of university life in Britain and the USA, atheistic chemists are usually considerably nicer to evangelicals than members of the Divinity Department. But we should remember, as we saw in the Introduction, that scholarship is not nearly as neutral as it proclaims itself to be.

So a document such as Caesar's *Gallic Wars* does not make spiritual and supernatural truth claims that demand a response from us. Julius Caesar does not say we are sinners in need of repentance. The New Testament does, and this, rather than the actual truth about the authenticity of the documents, is the *real* issue at stake here. When we talk about the reliability of the New Testament documents, this is always something we have to remember.

From a spiritual viewpoint, the authenticity of the New Testament is vital, especially for us as evangelicals.

How do we know what is true? Suppose I "feel" something to be so—does that make it true? What yardstick do we have to differentiate sincere feelings from absolute truth? To use the language of the postmodernists around us, how do we know that our narrative alone is true? What did Jesus really say, and to whom?

The evangelical answer to this is Scripture, and that is why, as Bible-based Christians, we must both believe in and defend the final revelation and authority of Scripture. Our reason for doing this therefore is not academic, a matter of historical debate, but is at the very core of why we are the kind of Christians that we claim to be as evangelicals.

On the one hand, we do have the Holy Spirit within us, guiding us and leading us. But how do we know whether what we sense inside us is genuinely from the Holy Spirit or not? How do we distinguish what might be a bright idea of our own or, even worse, a satanic temptation from an authentic prompting by the Holy Spirit within us?

The answer that Scripture itself gives is that everything we think or feel must be in full accord with what we know is God's proven Word to us, the Bible. We as evangelicals hold to the Holy Spirit inspiring Scripture. So if someone says, "The Holy Spirit is telling me . . ." we always have an entirely reliable way of testing that—what is in the Scriptures themselves. We can make mistakes, even well-meant and wholly sincere errors, but Scripture is never wrong.

We do not believe that the Holy Spirit dictated the words by rote, which is what the Muslims believe about the Koran. Each New Testament writer has clear literary styles of his own. So Luke, for example, reads differently from Paul. But what they both wrote was inspired by the Holy Spirit, so that the documents they composed are both true spiritually and without error factually.

Inerrancy, to use a technical term, is a subject over which there has been much discussion and heated debate in theological circles over many decades. But as the late Francis Schaeffer said in a speech in Switzerland back in 1974, "Inerrancy is the watershed of evangelicalism." You can be a Christian without believing in it, but not an evangelical. If the Bible includes mistakes, if the narrative/historical parts of it contain errors, how do we know that the spiritual side of the New Testament is true? Schaeffer quoted me in one of his books, referring to a personally delightful but theologically confused professor who gave lectures saying that he believed the Bible despite all its mistakes.

Many claim with total and genuine sincerity to be able to do this, and I do not doubt that they really do believe what they say. But by what authority can they say they believe, for example, in the ethics of Jesus while at the same time saying that our source for His ethical teaching, the Bible, is a human document filled with factual mistakes? I cannot see how you can have your cake and eat it too. So the defense

of Scripture is at the heart of what we know not just about the historical
background to Jesus and the New Testament but to who Jesus was as
God and Savior and all that He taught and stood for.

Liberal scholars might therefore claim to be objective—and label
evangelicals as biased—and be completely sincere in such belief. But
in fact the real difference is that we are open about our faith and the
way in which it shapes our thinking, whereas they are incorrect in
thinking themselves to be completely scholarly and objective. We
need to recognize their complete sincerity—they are not being two-
faced—but it is a sad self-deception nonetheless.

This is why, for example, they will deny that the person who is supposed to have written a book—John, say, or Peter—could have done
so. They cheerfully invent things like "the Johannine community,"
unnamed followers of John who decades or maybe centuries after his
death put together accounts of what they think he thought and then
wrote it up in his name.

Such critics also exclude from Scripture anything that they do not
believe in themselves. Modern writers, whether theologically liberal
professing Christians or outright atheists and agnostics, wholly reject
the supernatural. Twenty-first-century critics have beliefs that are
incompatible with belief in the supernatural of any kind. So nothing
that tells of miracles or says that Jesus believed Himself to be the Son
of God can be regarded as true or having actually taken place, in their
view. But such criticism does not say whether or not something really
happened or that a document is verifiably ancient.

But we believe that God inspired the individual authors to be both
accurate factually and spiritually, relaying the living Word of God to
those of us who have lived in the millennia since the New Testament
was written.

But having examined the spiritual context, we can as Christians
rejoice that so many authenticated documents do exist from so very
early on in the Christian church. This is an interesting contrast with
Islam, where no equivalent copies of the Koran exist with a date so
close to the founding of that faith. The earliest New Testament codices

or documents are much nearer to the origins of Christianity than the most ancient Korans are to the dawn of Islam.

Some fragments of the New Testament can be dated reliably to the end of the first century, to almost within the lifetime of the original authors. There are full copies of the New Testament—such as the Chester Beatty papyrus, from the early third century, which is, to take our earlier example, hundreds of years closer to its original than any of the documents written by Julius Caesar, whose authenticity no one doubts. Archaeology can be very supportive of the historicity of many passages in the New Testament, especially if conducted by experts open-minded enough to believe that events described in the Bible are capable of having taken place.

We as evangelicals, therefore, have no need to fear real scholarship, since it supports the claims of the Bible to be true. We should not reject authentic scholarship, archaeology, and similar academic studies simply because those who oppose Christianity use similar tools with which to attack the faith. Scholarship properly conducted is a wonderful encouragement to Christians and a superb apologetic tool in convincing nonbelievers to take the claims of the Bible seriously.

Creeds, Councils, and Conversions

B y the fourth century the Roman Empire had become far too large and unwieldy for one man to rule himself. The Empire was therefore split into two geographical units—the west, which was only to last until the end of the fifth century, and the east, which in different guises managed to survive until destroyed in 1453 by Muslim armies.

Each half had two rulers—an Augustus or senior emperor and a Caesar or junior ruler. While some dynasties were able to last a brief while, others hardly survived beyond their founder. Whether or not someone made it to Augustus status depended not so much on parentage but on brute force, cunning, and the ability to persuade large numbers of Roman legionaries to support his bid for power.

In 312, at a place not far from Rome called the Milvian Bridge, just such a battle took place. The victor was Constantine. The son of a minor ruler, he had been born in Britain, although of Roman ancestry, and had a similarly British-born mother, Helena. Beginning

his campaign in York, a town in northern Britain, he fought his way
to the Milvian Bridge and to victory.

Unusual for a pagan Roman, he attributed success to the Christian
God, saying that God had provided him with a message: "conquer
in this sign."

While it is incorrect to say that it was Constantine who made Christianity the official religion of the Roman Empire—that came later—he
declared it officially tolerated and therefore fully legal. Overnight
Christians went from being a persecuted faith to being the fashionable
religion of one of the most powerful rulers that the Roman Empire
had seen in a long time.

Historians have debated ever since whether Constantine converted
to a genuine faith or not, and at this vast distance it is impossible to
say. One can certainly hope so for his sake, but either way the effects
were dramatic.

Christianity, the faith of the emperor, was now able to spread legally.
Meetings that had hitherto been clandestine became overt, and com-
munication across the Empire, which had been difficult during times
of persecution, now became much easier to achieve.

It seems to me that while the end of persecution was good news—
who wants to be persecuted, after all—the link with the state would
prove disastrous. Christianity was now associated with the Roman Empire, and that meant that evangelism outside of the Empire, notably in
the powerful Sassanid Empire next door in Persia, became much more
difficult. People no longer considered Christianity as a faith in its own
right but instead perceived it as the faith of the Roman Empire.

An aside by a dyed-in-the-wool, theologically conservative,
Reformed-evangelical—but British—Christian: is there a similar
danger in the USA today if non-Christians link evangelical Christianity with the Republican Party and see Evangelicalism through not
spiritual but political lenses? I ask this because many have seen it as a
danger for faithful American evangelicals, and being solidly evangelical
myself but also, as a Briton, an outsider to U.S. politics, this causes
me legitimate concern.

One of the dangers of the new church-state link soon became apparent. The emperor, whose own theology was far from certain, now wanted uniformity within Christian ranks. While this was a good idea in and of itself—Christians had hitherto, because of persecution, not been able to travel and meet in person to discuss such things among themselves—the fact that the emperor called the first Council at the town of Nicea, near the new Roman capital of Constantinople, shows the way in which the new wind was blowing.

So in 325 we had the first of the so-called Ecumenical Councils of the Church, meetings that over the next few hundred years were to prove doctrinally important and are also of vital significance to both Roman Catholics and to Orthodox churches today (with western and eastern Christianity diverging only on whether or not some of the later Councils were equally binding).

What Is the Church?

All of this naturally therefore poses the question: what is the church? This issue strikes a chord with us even in the twenty-first century.

In our own time Christians legitimately differ on how they interpret this question. Anglicans in Britain, Calvinist Church of Scotland members, and State Church Lutherans in Denmark are all members of churches that have formal links with their respective states. Evangelicals in these denominations sometimes defend this, saying that the fact of Establishment, as it is called in England and Scotland, enables real Christians to argue that Christianity does and should have a formal role in how the country is run and that biblical perspectives must always be taken into account.

However, if one looks at the USA, where there is specific separation of church and state, one sees a country where Christianity is vibrant, growing, and dynamic as opposed to the far smaller churches, of all descriptions, in countries such as Britain and Denmark—and in the latter the number of Bible-believing evangelicals is tiny.

Furthermore, one of the spiritually strongest and rapidly expanding churches in the world today is in the People's Republic of China, where, as in the days of the pagan Roman Empire, Christianity is persecuted, even if there is a veneer of tolerance for those who are prepared to register their churches with the authorities.

So in terms of spiritual growth, dynamism, and overall health, which is stronger—the church in countries where it is linked to the state, such as England, Scotland, and Denmark, or nations where it is not, such as the USA, China, and Nigeria? According to some statistics there are twenty times as many *actual church-attending members* of the Anglican Communion in Nigeria than in England itself. However, only one twenty-fifth of nominal Anglicans ever attend church in Britain. So the real ratio is twenty million Nigerians, most of whom are evangelical, to one million English, half of whom are evangelical.

This argument took place in the fourth century but did not fully occur again, as we shall see, until the Reformation. Is the church the gathered people of God on earth from all nations, tribes, and languages and divided on Sunday into local congregations, or is there now such a thing as a Christian nation? And if a Christian nation is possible, what role does the state have in enforcing Christian values, even in matters such as compulsory church attendance on Sundays?

I will discuss this more fully when we look at the Reformation and see the rise of non-state-linked denominations, of which the Baptists have been the most prominent since they began in the decades after the dawn of Protestantism.

But from the beginning there were devout Christians who were very unhappy with the way in which the leadership of the church was becoming increasingly enmeshed with the Roman emperor and the tendency of emperors to interfere in what had hitherto been solely church decisions.

In particular a group called the Donatists asked the question, "What does the emperor have to do with the church?"

This body of North African Christians originated with Bishop Donatus, after whom they were named. The issue that triggered the dissent was when Donatus was asked to approve as a fellow bishop someone who had during the persecution buckled and denied being a Christian. In the first three centuries—as in lands today where Christians are under severe pressure—many had done this out of human fear, while inwardly keeping true to their Christian profession. While this is understandable from a human viewpoint—however regrettable—it equally understandably irked other Christians who held firm to their faith outwardly as well, even though to do so often meant certain and painful death. To the latter group—of whom Donatus was one—only those who had kept true under persecution and had refused to deny their faith were eligible for Christian office.

This was not the policy of the government, who wanted Christians of all kinds to come together whether or not they had denied anything before the persecution ended. Not only that, but with the emperor himself at least professing Christianity, fashionable society and those with political or military ambitions were now also joining the church, and their motives were inevitably suspect. If leadership was confined to those who had stayed faithful under the threat of death, then there could be certainty that such people were genuine Christians and deserved their high office.

The Donatists therefore split off, forming a pure church of their own. Needless to say, they were persecuted. This time the persecutors were not pagans but those also declaring themselves to be Christians. Even the great St. Augustine of Hippo would oppose the Donatist separatists in his lifetime.

This remains a key issue in the church in China today, with those in the underground or unregistered churches tending often to look down on what they think is the unacceptable compromise of fellow Christians who join the state-approved Three-Self Patriotic Church. From what I gather there are real evangelicals in the latter—they are by no means all theological liberals—and it is in any case very hard for Christians like us who live in the freedom of the West to judge what it must be like to be a believer in such unenviable circumstances.

But as we shall see, with the arrival of the Reformation, free or dissenting churches soon arose that, like the Donatists, refused to have anything to do with the state churches. Luther, Calvin, Knox, and Cranmer all belonged to churches where the state/church link was maintained, earning themselves the name of the Magisterial Reformers. It took a long time and many decades of one godly group of Protestants persecuting another and also Catholics and Protestants putting one another to death before the pre-Constantine separation was once again regarded as an acceptable option for believing Christians. Over 1,300 years of church/state links were beginning.

So when church leaders met in Nicea in 325, everyone wanted to work out what official Christian doctrine now was.

Contrary to the nonsense perpetrated in novels such as *The Da Vinci Code*—against which many excellent books have been written (such as *The Gospel Code: A Critique of the Da Vinci Code* by Ben Witherington III)—there was *already* a general doctrinal consensus on issues and key doctrines and on which books were legitimately canonical and thus part of the Bible and which were not.

But certain doctrinal issues remained, including some that we take so much for granted today that we forget that such matters could ever have been in dispute. In particular these were important for the Greek-speaking majority since Greek is a very precise language in which subtle nuances exist that simpler Latin speakers would miss. Here the key debate was between the followers of Arius (c. 250–336), who denied that Christ was both fully God and fully man, and those of Athanasius (296–373), who realized that Christ was both and whose views prevailed not only in 325 but among the vast majority of Christians ever since.

Arians still exist under other names, including, for example, the Coptic Orthodox Church in Egypt and the Orthodox Church in Ethiopia.

This was no mere academic debate. If Christ was not fully man, He could not have been our proper representative on the cross for our sins. And if He were not fully God, then He would not have been equal with the Father and the Holy Spirit. He had to be both God and man, and the Council duly endorsed the correct position on that issue.

Athanasius had won, but one of Constantine's successors, Constantius, was an Arian, and after a time when Arians were persecuted, those, like Athanasius, the bishop of the mainly Greek Egyptian city of Alexandria, who believed the truth were now themselves persecuted. (As Jerome, the great Bible translator, quipped ironically during this time, "We are all Arians now." Needless to say, in Jerome's case he was only joking.)

This was to be a regrettable pattern that lasted for centuries to come, with Christians using the power of the state to persecute those who disagreed with them doctrinally, even if, like Athanasius or later Augustine or Luther, we might agree doctrinally with those carrying out the persecution rather than with its victims.

For a brief while there was even a pagan emperor again—Julian the Apostate, who died supposedly with the words, "Man of Galilee, you have won."

Thankfully, the Arians lost in the end, though it was a close situation since many of the Germanic tribes who invaded and destroyed the western half of the Roman Empire in the fifth century had converted to Arianism.

Arius was an Egyptian who taught that while Christ was the joint creator of the universe, he was nonetheless not God. He was a created being like us, albeit one with an extra-special status.

His views were therefore outside the mainstream of Christianity altogether, not some view over which Christians could legitimately differ, such as on baptism or separation. (Arians were thus substantially different from Donatists, whose spiritual views were entirely within Christian orthodoxy.)

Inevitably there were those, as now, who wanted a compromise that kept everyone happy. In the Greek the differential between the two positions—Arian and scriptural—was in fact just one Greek letter. If Jesus was part of the Trinity—the biblical view—He and the Father were of the *same* substance (*homoousion* in Greek). The compromise version was one letter different: *homoiousion*. But this means "of *like* substance," which suggests that Christ is like but not fully part of the Trinity. This compromise was clearly a false view, however well-intentioned in terms of making peace between the factions. But it took not a few Councils of the Church and the now famous Athanasian Creed (named for Athanasius) and Nicene Creed (after Nicea) to sort it all out.

Since the Nicene Creed is still used today, in Protestant as well as in Catholic and Orthodox churches, it might be worth quoting it in full, so we can see the historic roots of the creeds that so influenced the subsequent history of the Christian Church.

> We believe in one God, the Father Almighty, Maker of heaven and earth, and of all things visible and invisible.
>
> And in one Lord Jesus Christ, the only-begotten Son of God,
> Begotten by the Father before all ages,
> Light of Light, True God of True God, begotten not made, of *one substance* [emphasis added] with the Father, through whom all things were made;
> Who for us men and for our salvation came down from the heavens, and was made flesh of the Holy Spirit, and of the Virgin Mary, and became man;
> And was crucified for us under Pontius Pilate, and suffered and was buried, and rose again on the third day according to the Scriptures;
> And ascended into the heavens, and sits on the right hand of the Father;
> And comes again with glory to judge the living and the dead, of whose Kingdom there shall be no end.
> And in the Holy Spirit, the Lord and the Life-Giver, that proceeds from the Father, who with Father and Son is worshipped together and glorified together, who spoke through the Prophets;
> In one Holy Catholic [= universal] and Apostolic Church;
> We acknowledge one baptism unto the remission of sins.
> We look for a resurrection of the dead, and the life of the age to come.

Strange though it may seem today, all this was the subject of conversation as much among ordinary people as among intellectuals and leaders. One of the latter who found this out was the great fourth-century bishop Gregory of Nyssa (330–395), who, as one can see from his dates, lived in the generation after all the initial discussions.

One day he was walking down the street of the capital and discovered:

> If you ask anyone in Constantinople for change, he will start discussing with you whether the Son is begotten or unbegotten. If you ask about the quality of bread, you will get the answer, "The Father is greater, the Son is less!" If you suggest taking a bath, you will be told, "There was nothing before the Son was created."

Gregory was also an eminent theologian. He and his brother Basil the Great (330–379) and their colleague Gregory of Nazianzus (329–389) became known as the Cappadocian Fathers, from the part of Anatolia in which they lived.

There was one downside to the victory of orthodoxy on the subject of the Trinity over the Arian heresy, one that has dire consequences for us in the twenty-first century. It is, I would argue, a direct result of the church's acceptance of Constantine's linking both church and state.

Today we would not agree with Unitarians, the nearest equivalent of the Arians of that time. But we would not jail them or put them to death. However, in the fourth to sixth centuries matters were different. Athanasius himself was, as we saw, exiled under the Arian Emperor Constantius from his see in Alexandria and then reinstalled when a different emperor reverted to the biblical view. So in the end it was the Arians who ended up being persecuted for over two hundred years by the emperors for being heretics. In 381 Arianism was finally outlawed, and it remained so thereafter.

By this era the Western Roman Empire had vanished. So we now call the emperors by the anachronistic name of Byzantine emperors, although officially they saw themselves as the legitimate Roman emperors, right down to the Muslim conquest of the remnant of Constantinople in 1453.

Islam began in the seventh century, and that would have dire consequences. The local supporters of heretical sects had long been angered
at being persecuted by the more orthodox Byzantine government. Muslims did not differentiate between one group of professing Christians
and another. So when they conquered what was then the Christian
Middle East from 632 onward, they gave full religious toleration (but
not what we would regard as human rights) to Christians of all stripes,
mainstream and Arian alike. This pleased the Arians since they could
now worship freely under Islamic rule in a way that had been impossible under a nominally Christian Byzantine government. This was to
prove tragic in the long run since what was once an overwhelmingly
Christian region is today predominantly Islamic. We are so used to
thinking of places such as Iraq (then called Mesopotamia), Egypt,
and Syria as Muslim, we forget that they were once the heartland of
the Christian world.

In the fourth century one could still speak of a single Christian
world. But in the fifth century, when Germanic and similar tribes invaded and conquered the western part of the Roman Empire, centered
on Rome, the slow division began between Western, Latin-speaking
Christianity, which we now call Catholicism, and that of the East
Roman Empire, which lasted, later in severely attenuated form, for
another thousand years and which we would now regard as the heartland of Orthodox Christianity.

Theodosius the Great (reigned 379–395), for example, still ruled
over large parts of Italy, with a capital in Milan as well as the main
center in Constantinople. By 394 paganism was officially outlawed,
though many parts of Europe continued, alongside nominal Catholic
faith, to practice what we would now regard as pagan customs at least
until the twentieth century, especially in the remoter regions. (The
Latin word *paganus* literally means "country dweller," and in remote
places paganism, or "folk practices" as anthropologists would call it,
lasted a very long time.)

Theodosius, while uniquely powerful, was willing to be rebuked
when he acted out of line. After massacring rebels in Thessaloniki (the

original town in which the Thessalonians of Bible times once lived) in 390, he went to Milan. There he was publicly remonstrated by the bishop, the great theologian Ambrose (339–397), one of the ablest combatants of the Arian heresy.

After Theodosius, no one Roman emperor was powerful enough to impose his will on the full extent of the old Empire. Britain vanished from Roman rule at the start of the fifth century, and by the end of that period Rome itself was under barbarian rule.

As we have seen, there was some intellectual difference between Greek and Latin thought, with the Greeks more prone to abstraction than the more down-to-earth Latin thinkers. Whereas in the past the leading theologians and intellectuals had come from the Greek-speaking eastern half, we now see the emergence of perhaps the greatest of all early theologians, Augustine of Hippo, a man of Berber ethnicity (the main minority in North Africa, now Arabic-speaking and Muslim) but who thought and wrote in Latin.

The fact that the region from which he came—Hippo—is in what is now Tunisia should give us pause for thought. It was then over-whelmingly Christian but is now an overwhelmingly Muslim country, having been conquered in the wave of Islamic invasions that began in the seventh century. The world we live in now is a truly very different place.

Augustine—St. Augustine to Catholics—lived from 354 to 430. He was regarded in the Middle Ages as the greatest of all the Fathers of the Church, and because of the way in which Calvin rediscovered so much of his thought—on predestination, for instance—he is given due reverence among Protestants today as well, especially those of Reformed persuasion.

Augustine had a pagan father and a Christian mother. After an early life of misbehavior and dissolution, during which he also studied the classics and philosophy, he was then gloriously converted, at the age of thirty-two, in 386. He was ordained in 391 and became Bishop of Hippo in 396, where he stayed for the rest of his life.

His still-read *Confessions* tell us about his early life, and they remain a powerful evangelistic tool to this day. As one reads them it is clear how much humanity has *not* changed. While we live in a high-tech, twenty-first-century world, the human, moral, ethical, and other problems with which Augustine wrestled are still with us in full measure. Technology changes; people do not.

His other famous work, *The City of God*, was written in 410, the year of the first major sacking of Rome by the barbarians. This event shocked the civilized world, Augustine not the least among them. While Alaric, the barbarian leader, did not finally keep Rome, it was a blow from which the western half of the Empire would never recover. In his book, therefore, Augustine contrasts Christian truth with the falsehood of the pagans and in the process gives us a fascinating insight on how Christians at the time saw the historical process unfolding.

Augustine made several major contributions to theology. One of these was the *filioque* controversy, the issue that was eventually to lead to a permanent split seven centuries later (in 1054) between Orthodox East and Catholic West. Augustine, like Catholics and Protestants ever since, believed that the Holy Spirit proceeded from *both the Father and the Son* (the Latin *filioque* means "and the Son"). The Orthodox Church then as now rejected such a belief, and the rift was already underway during Augustine's lifetime.

But it is above all in the field of *soteriology*—how we are saved by God, the mechanism through which Jesus as our Savior (*soter*) saves us—that Augustine is best remembered.

To those of us from the Reformed end of the evangelical spectrum, all Augustine was doing was simply expounding what Paul teaches in Ephesians and Romans—a doctrinal outlook that was to be rediscovered, as we shall see, by Luther as much as by Calvin during the Reformation twelve hundred or so years later.

God, Augustine realized, is not sitting passively in heaven waiting to see if anyone chooses to become a Christian. Rather, God in love reached out to us through Jesus Christ on the cross. Becoming a Christian, therefore, is not an act of human whim but a process in which God is not merely active but is also the initiator, choosing those whom He in his perfect love and mercy will save.

This is still a controversial issue today with some Christians, alas. Those who follow the Dutch thinker Arminius—of whom we will say more later—think that Augustine invented this doctrine and that Calvin continued it. While I would find it hard to see how fellow evangelicals could have such a different reading of the Pauline epistles—not to mention many other parts of both the Old and New Testaments—it is true that many evangelicals today disagree with the way in which Augustine, and millions of Reformed Christians since, have interpreted what seems to us the clear teaching of Scripture. It does show, too, though that what seem to be ancient debates—Augustine died over fifteen hundred years ago—are very relevant to us as Christians today.

In the fifth century heresies had not been altogether disproved. In Antioch, which was still a major Christian city, there arose a bishop named Nestorius who denied what the church had decided at Nicea. This had to be dealt with in a new series of Councils, first at Ephesus in 431 and finally at Chalcedon in 451, when the overwhelming view that Jesus truly is both divine and human finally prevailed. Many Orthodox churches still call themselves Chalcedonian after that Council in 451, especially those based in the USA.

In the west most Christians agreed with Chalcedon—though in 476, when Rome was finally overwhelmed by the barbarians, those holding to biblical theology had a difficult time for quite a while since many of the invaders were Arian and took a while to understand the truth. One of the leading experts at Chalcedon was the Bishop of Rome, Leo the Great (known to Catholics as St. Leo I), who helped draw up the successful formulae. Since Rome fell to the barbarians twenty-five years later, this was the last time a Western leader would contribute in an important way to a major Christian council.

In the east the controversy continued for some while, and today thousands of professing Christians in the Middle East and East Africa follow the unorthodox view. They believe that Christ had only one nature and are consequently sometimes referred to as Monophysites, *mono* in Greek meaning "one" or "single." Today's Copts are such a group, as is the main historic Orthodox Church in Ethiopia.

Needless to say, the Byzantine authorities soon began to persecute the Nestorians, as Nestorius's followers were called. However, in this case the persecution was a major spur to evangelism and to bringing their version of Christianity well beyond the borders of the Roman Empire, as far afield as China, thousands of miles away across hard terrain.

The fact that those with a biblical theology did not evangelize beyond Roman borders is a terrible indictment of mainstream Christianity. Orthodox Christians in the east would eventually begin the evangelism of eastern Europe, and the Cyrillic alphabet used by Russians, Bulgarians, and Serbs today is a tribute to the missionary endeavors of two brave Orthodox monks, Cyril and Methodius. Similarly, from the sixth century onward Roman Catholic missionaries began, over the course of a thousand years, to evangelize western and central Europe, with the final pagan nation, the Lithuanians, eventually converting to Christianity by the fourteenth century.

But at no stage did either Orthodox or Catholic missionaries go beyond the borders of Europe, to evangelize, say, Africa to the south or the lands of Persia and China to the east. This was not the case with the Nestorians, however. Driven by persecution outside the Empire, they settled first in Persia, the empire that was Rome's ancient enemy, and then reached as far as China itself, where in the days of the great Tang Dynasty large Nestorian congregations and even cathedrals were to be found all over the vast Chinese empire.

The Nestorians were still there during the much later visits of Marco Polo and during the Mongol invasions in the time of Genghis and Kublai Khan. Historians reckon that what finally ended the Nestorians was the decision in the thirteenth century of the Mongol rulers of Persia—the Il-Khans—to convert to Islam. So while Monophysites exist today in Egypt and Ethiopia and in some of the smaller groups in the Middle East, the Nestorians as such are no more.

After 476 the church in the west was in effect on its own, although some parts of Italy were conquered from time to time by Byzantine rulers. The Bishop of Rome therefore developed an importance that the holders of that office had not enjoyed before. Until then all the leading Christian officials had been in the east, the patriarchs of great cities such as Alexandria and Antioch. The Pope, as we now call the Roman bishop, had no predominance and was very much one among equals in the Councils of the church.

But after the barbarian conquest, the Roman bishop was in effect the last remnant of the old western half of the Roman Empire, the one continuation of the civilization that had existed before the invaders destroyed it and took western Europe into what some historians still refer to as the Dark Ages.

Catholics would, of course, disagree with such an interpretation. But I think it is fair to say that the Papacy owes its supremacy to accident rather than to anything else.

The other key thing to remember is that in the east, the part of the Roman Empire that lasted until 1453 (with a gap of a few decades in the thirteenth century), the emperor remained far more important than the church patriarchs, a direct legacy of Constantine and the way in which the state could prevail even doctrinally over the church.

This was not the case in the chaotic west, where what had once been the Roman Empire was now a myriad host of smaller and rival kingdoms, all fighting with each other. And until the crowning of the European Frankish leader Charlemagne (= *Carolus Magnus* or Charles the Great) in 800, there was thus no rival for the Pope to keep him in check.

In due time the Popes even became secular rulers, with the political results that we will see in the next chapter. Right up until 1870 the Popes were secular rulers of what they called the Patrimony of St. Peter, which until 1859 or 1860 was also called the Papal States. While Catholics would again disagree, there is no doubt that this is why the vast majority of Popes have been Italian, until Pope John Paul II in 1978, since the Popes were Italian rulers alongside such now long extinct titles as the Grand Dukes of Tuscany or the Dukes of Savoy. Even today the tiny area of Vatican City is a country in its own right, ever since the deal between the Italian Fascist leader Mussolini and the Pope in 1929. All this is a legacy of the chaos left in the fifth century by the barbarian invasions and the ability of the Bishops of Rome to exploit their spiritual office for wider political ends.

A few former Roman territories were able to survive spiritually independent of Rome, and this was the case in the British Isles until the Synod of Whitby in 664, when the Roman Pope was finally able to prevail over the local Christians.

In this instance the church that survived the barbarian invasions of Britain in the early fifth century was Celtic—the race to which the original indigenous peoples probably belonged and from whom today's Irish and Welsh peoples descend directly.

The invaders—Angles, Saxons, and Jutes from present-day northern Germany and Denmark—were overwhelmingly pagan. So the Celtic Christians had to accomplish two things—first, to survive at all, which in itself was hard, and, second, to do all possible to convert those invaders to Christian faith. What is interesting to note here is that the Irish, who did so much to keep British Christianity alive, were a people who had never themselves been under Roman rule.

Not all the Irish had been Christian, and one of the most famous Christians of this period is Patrick (390–460), an aristocrat of mixed Roman and British descent who helped spearhead the evangelism of Ireland in his lifetime, especially after 432 when he went there as a missionary bishop.

Much of what remains from the Dark Ages is from Irish Celtic sources, including, for example, the wonderful illuminated manuscript from a few centuries later, the *Book of Kells*, which historians think was produced around 800.

The Celtic Church was primarily monastic and certainly was not hierarchical in the manner of the Roman Church with its layers of ecclesiastical authority. Celtic missionaries were soon active on the continent of Europe, with Columbanus (543–615) bringing Chris-

tianity back to Gaul after the barbarian invasions there, and his col-
laborator Gall (550–645) taking the Christian faith to what is now
Switzerland.

"Celtic spirituality" has become very fashionable in recent years, especially among those of a New Age persuasion who want to have some
of the mystical elements of Christianity—as they perceive it—without
the need for repentance and thus a complete change of lifestyle. This
is, I think, because many of the Celts lived close to nature—in the
north of England, for example, often surrounded by seagulls on remote
islands—and therefore twenty-first-century followers of "Deep Ecol-
ogy" today see them as kindred spirits communing intimately with
an unspoiled environment.

While it is possible that some Celtic Christians did come peril-
ously near Pantheism, they mainly stayed very much to the right side
of the line. And since the works of some great Celtic thinkers such as
Cuthbert are still in print, it is possible to read what they wrote *in toto*
and not pick and mix as New-Agers are prone to do.

By the sixth century the era of Celtic isolation was over—the Popes
had rediscovered the British Isles.

English slaves were traded extensively all over Europe, and one
of the most eminent of the early Popes, Gregory the Great (reigned
590–604), spotted some of them in the slave market in Rome. He
is legendarily supposed to have said, on seeing them, that they were
"Angels not Angles." While such apocryphal stories are nice to believe,
sadly there is no proof he ever uttered such words.

But be that as it may, he certainly realized both that England (as
it was now beginning to be called—the land of the Angles) needed
evangelism and that the Christians there should be under Roman
control.

As a consequence, he began the evangelism of England from a
Catholic point of view. In 597 St. Augustine of Canterbury (who lived
to 605) was sent as a missionary to the kingdom in the southeastern
part of England nearest to the Continent. This was the Jutish kingdom
of Kent—the Jutes being descended from those coming from Jutland,

a peninsula now part of both Denmark and Germany. One of the key towns in Kent was Canterbury, and Augustine became the first Archbishop of Canterbury during his stay—a post that has existed down to the present time, which explains why the spiritual head of the Church of England has his cathedral so far to the south of the country and outside of London.

Slowly but surely, as the Venerable Bede, the historian of the conversion of England, explains in his famous history, the Roman missionaries worked their way up the country, slowly evangelizing the different kingdoms and bringing the gospel to the pagan Angles, Saxons, and Jutes.

For a while the Celtic Church was able to exist alongside the Roman. But the Celts did not agree to papal supremacy, and in some small doctrinal areas—such as how a monk should shave or *tonsure* his head and on how to fix the date of Easter—they disagreed strongly. As was to become sadly inevitable, the local kings, and as time went by the kings-in-chief or *bretwaldas*, became involved in internal church disagreements. In 664 one of these, Oswy, king of the northern English kingdom of Northumberland (from which area George Washington's ancestors were to come), summoned both sides to a major Synod at the Abbey of Whitby, the ruins of which can still be seen today. At Whitby the Romans won over the Celts, and England became part of the Roman Catholic Church down to the Reformation in the 1530s.

The then Pope, Vitalian, was careful not to humiliate the Celts and so deliberately chose in 668 a new archbishop who was not from Rome but was in fact a Greek from Tarsus, the town of the apostle Paul. This was Theodore (602–690), who brought along with him an African, Hadrian (died 709), to help him. This gave the British church an exotic Afro-Asian flavor and marks the return of British Christianity to the mainstream. Soon British Christians such as Winifrith of Crediton (680–754) were active in missionary evangelism of the Continent—Winifrith, for example, taking the name of Boniface, and, under that new calling, setting off to evangelize what is now Germany, founding a still existing monastery in Fulda and ending his days as the Archbishop of Mainz.

THREE

Medieval Christianity

T his chapter will look at the Christian church predominantly
in the West, and in particular at the years between the fall of
Rome in 476 and the dawn of the Reformation in 1517.

As that is a major time span for a single chapter, we will look at
that thousand-year period thematically. We will look at the Crusades
and then at the nature of the church itself, including how ordinary
Christians lived in that period about which we as evangelical Christians often know rather little.

The Roman Empire survived in the east until 1453, something
that will be important to remember later on when we look at its split
with the west in 1054 and the disastrous episode known today as the
Crusades.

However, in western and central Europe, the great edifice of Roman
power collapsed, with nothing solid to succeed it until 800. In that year
the ruler of the Franks, Charles the Great (*Carolus Magnus* in Latin;
Charlemagne), declared himself to be Holy Roman Emperor, a title
that was to last for over a thousand years, down to 1806.

One key point needs to be made for us as evangelical Christians: do we believe that no one was saved, born again, and went to heaven in that thousand-year period? I will discuss this in more detail later, but it is important to contemplate this theologically. We rightly revere, look back to, and defend the Reformation. But in so doing we need to be careful about saying that there were no Christians over so long a prior time frame. Surely we cannot say that whatever the doctrinal quirks of the medieval church, and we will not deny them, no one was redeemed for over a millennium.

What secular historians call Late Antiquity—the time between the fall of Rome and the origins of the Holy Roman Empire—was a period of slow but steady conversions as pagan peoples heard the gospel for the first time and became Christians. We have looked at some of this already in considering how England became Christian, and the same gradual process took place in other parts of western Europe as well. (Central Europe, as we shall see, remained pagan for far longer.) Brave monks would venture into the great forests, some would be martyred, and others proved successful, with one of the biggest tribes, the Franks, converting around 496.

When we talk of peoples becoming Christian, we need to recall that similar large-scale conversions of people groups still occur, often now in less developed parts of the world. We may feel more comfortable with individual conversions, and one does wonder at the authenticity of so many in a single ethnic or similar group professing faith simultaneously. Yet it does seem that such things can be genuine if God is truly behind them.

Also growing rapidly at this time was the power of the Bishop of Rome, the Pope, since it was his office that was the one major remnant from the days of the Roman Empire, along with the order and stability that empire brought with it. Now that western Europe was cut off politically, culturally, and increasingly theologically from the other powerful centers of ancient Christianity, those who deemed themselves the Pope's equals were far removed, and the Pope's power in western Europe grew accordingly.

Not only that but in the early seventh century a series of events took place that changed the world forever, right down to the terrorism we face in the West to this very day. I am referring to the rise of a new faith, that of Islam.

I have dealt with Islam far more extensively in other books I have written. Here I look at its impact on the early church, which was profound and in ways that we have, alas, forgotten all too easily today.

When Iraq was invaded in 2003, a group entered western and Christian consciousness about whom we have failed to remember all too much. These were the Assyrian and Chaldean Christian minorities in Iraq, who have been professing Christianity since the dawn of our faith two thousand years ago. We forget that there have been, and in some places still are, Arab Christians who have lived in the Middle East since the missionary journeys of Paul back in the first century. Not only that, but until the seventh century the majority of people living in what is now Iraq, Syria, Jordan, Israel, and Egypt were all professing Christians of one kind or another. That was also true of other parts of the world, such as North Africa (Augustine was a Berber in ethnic origin).

All of this was dramatically altered by the rise of Islam.

In 610 an Arab trader, Muhammad, had a series of visions that he claimed to be from God. Over the course of the rest of his life, until his death in 632, he continued to claim such visions, and at the same time he engaged in spreading his beliefs by a mix of evangelism and military conquest. His four main successors, the Rightly Guided Caliphs, took Islam well beyond the borders of Arabia, stopped only by a Frankish army in southern France one hundred years after Muhammad's death, at a battle between Tours and Poitiers in 732.

Areas that we now think of as inexorably Islamic were once Christian, and this includes, as we have seen, most of the Fertile Crescent and northern Africa. Spain itself was invaded in 711, most of it then conquered, and what is now France would have been too, with towns such as Narbonne being briefly under Muslim rule. So too was Sicily, and the Italian mainland, the seat of the Papacy, came close to being conquered as well. The Christian survival of most of the West by a whisker was, to use a British expression, a "near run thing."

Many authors of different persuasions have demonstrated that Islam held the balance of military power against the West until well into the seventeenth century, until around 1683, when, as we shall see, an Islamic army failed for the second time to capture Vienna. So for well over a thousand years, roughly 632 to 1683, western Europe lay in permanent fear of Islamic conquest, with much of Spain and Portugal being under Muslim rule for seven hundred years. Eastern Europe was part of an Islamic empire, the Muslim Ottoman Turks, from the fourteenth century right up until the twentieth, in the memory of some still living. Russia, too, was under Muslim/Mongol rule for centuries, in the shape of the Golden Horde.

Soon we will look at the Crusades, the period of the West in which soldiers, often under papal authority, would invade countries—from Spain, southern France, and the Baltic and on to the most famous of them in the Middle East. Here it is important to remember that *jihad*, the Islamic term for "holy war," is a Muslim term, not a Christian one. Islamic armies, for example, seized Jerusalem in 638, ruling over that area until 1099, and again, with gaps, from the 1180s until 1917. And although the invading Muslim armies did not force anyone to convert to Islam—an important point to remember—Christians and Jews were under legal disadvantage, or *dhimmi* status, in some cases right up to and including the twenty-first century.

Islam, even secular writers now think, is a kind of Jewish heresy mixed with much misunderstood elements of Christianity. (Again, I have written more extensively about this elsewhere.) It is in our own day the only other major international, cross-cultural, missionary, monotheistic faith. It is, as one Muslim writer has realized, the only other claimant to universal religious truth, a situation that author Bassam Tibi calls "a clash of universalisms."

From a spiritual point of view, this means that in many parts of today's world, it is *the* major rival to the other rapidly spreading mono-theistic faith, Christianity. In areas from Nigeria to Indonesia this often entails much violence as Christians find themselves sometimes literally under fire.

We do not have to believe that most of Islam is violent to find all this very disturbing. We can believe that many Muslims are genuinely moderate in their faith, believing, for example, that *jihad* is now no longer holy war but the internal spiritual struggle to be a better Muslim. Many Muslims today indeed abhor violence, especially since they feel that it besmirches the name of their religion in the eyes of the West. But in terms of competition for souls in many parts of the globe, Islam is the great spiritual opponent of our faith, even if its means are wholly pacific. Islam came to Indonesia, for example, mainly by trade and peaceful missionary endeavor, not by conquest.

The Crusades and the post-9/11 global rise of militant Islam and the discussion they still create embody perhaps one of the biggest changes in how we view the past since the first edition of this book came out in 1998.

On the one hand, I do not believe that 9/11 changed the whole world—much of it had long been engaged in a spiritual battle with Islam or with a physical struggle against that religion's militant wing. But on the other hand, the events of 2001 have at least alerted the country with the most Christians living in it, the USA, to the epic contest that has been waged for decades between those who spread the true faith of Christ and those who believe in its Islamic imitation. Whatever our political views on the way in which the war against terror is being waged, we can all be engaged in prayer for our sisters and brothers in Christ on the spiritual front lines against Islam, whether that struggle is pacific or not.

We now arrive naturally at the period in which the West decided to strike back against Islam, by sending not missionaries but armed soldiers who came not with the Bible but with a sword.

The actual period of the Crusades lasted just two centuries—from Pope Urban's proclamation in France of the first official Crusade in 1095 and the successful capture of Jerusalem in 1099 and the final expulsion of the last Crusaders from their toehold in the Holy Land, Acre, in 1291.

The Crusades, in other words, ended well over seven centuries ago. Yet to many people, especially in the Islamic Middle East, it seems as if they happened last week. Christians in the West are still being asked to "apologize" for the Crusades by Muslims, and after 9/11 there have, regrettably I feel, even been evangelicals who now think that these monstrosities were a good thing that we as Western Christians ought to defend. Osama bin Laden has called George W. Bush the chief crusader, and many on both sides of the war against global terrorism see that conflict as part of the ongoing battle between Islam and Christianity, something that many believe was at the heart of the Crusades.

This book, as is obvious by now, is written from an unashamedly evangelical and Protestant Christian perspective. I have already condemned the aggressive side of Islam, the military version of *jihad* that saw a century of active military aggression against Christian peoples from Iraq to Spain. But I think it is vital to begin by saying that from an evangelical, biblical, theological, and spiritually accurate standpoint, we cannot possibly even begin to defend the Crusades since they embody the kind of warped Christianity from which the great Reformers freed us centuries ago. While we should utterly oppose the evils of Islamic extremism, countering such vile doctrines by defending medieval knights who slaughtered innocent women and children in cold blood in the name of a seriously heretical version of Christian faith is not something that we as evangelicals should ever contemplate.

I have written extensively about this in books for both the secular and the Christian marketplace, notably *A Brief History of the Middle East* and *Christians, Muslims, and Islamic Rage* respectively. Here I am discussing it in the context of Christian history as a whole.

Let us look at two mistakes people often make when considering the Crusades, one historical/secular and the other spiritual.

We tend to look at the Crusades in isolation, and only at those that took place in the Middle East. We forget that other Crusades took place over the course of centuries in Spain and that some of the most bloodthirsty happened not in Palestine but in southern France, with one group of white Europeans slaughtering another.

Historically, therefore, only to consider one set of Crusades—those in the Middle East from 1099–1291—is a major error. Secular historians now put these in a much wider context of a history of armed struggle against the enemies of the church.

Popes would on occasion even have crusades against purely domestic opponents, which outraged people such as Dante, as this was seen as a serious abuse of what crusading meant.

The first of these other crusades began long before Urban sent western European warriors against the Muslim occupiers of Jerusalem. This was the Reconquest, or *Reconquista* in Spanish, the centuries-long (711–1492) reconquest of Spain from the Islamic armies that had conquered most of it in the period 711–732. The Muslim invaders, as we saw, but for the Battle of Tours/Poitiers in 732 would have successfully seized most of western Europe as well.

While a strongly Christian element in the recapture of Spain was inevitable, much of the reality of the reconquest was nationalist—Spaniards (or, more historically speaking, Castilians, Aragonese, and Portuguese) reclaiming their own territory from alien rule. Some leaders, such as Rodrigo, "El Cid," would play both sides against each other, and it was not a simple Christian vs. Muslim struggle in the nearly eight centuries over which it took place. Its effect on Spain was unfortunate. Spain, more than any other Catholic country, embraced the Inquisition, as we shall see, and Protestant Christianity, especially its evangelical version, was not made fully legal until as recently as the 1970s. To this day Spain remains one of the countries most impervious to Protestants.

The other predominantly nationalist war that turned into a kind of religious crusade was fought in what we now call Poland and the Baltic. The Germanic peoples were spreading east—the *Drang Nach Osten* that continued until World War II. Since the local Slavic tribes were predominantly pagan until comparatively far into the Middle Ages, the German campaigns took on the guise of a crusade to mask what was in fact an ethnic campaign of conquest. When the Poles and other central European peoples converted, the essentially nationalist element of the German conquerors—principally the Teutonic Knights—came into the open.

Both of these two wars—one of liberation and one of conquest—succeeded. So too did the Albigensian Crusade in the thirteenth century. Here it was one group of western Europeans against another, northern French Catholics fighting southern French Cathar heretics. Much of the south—today's Languedoc—had converted to a strange Manichean heresy called Catharism, an early medieval form of Gnosticism and a European version of the ancient Persian Zoroastrian religion.

Here the Popes had a twin track approach. The Dominican Order had a major role in preaching orthodox Christian faith (albeit in its medieval Catholic form), and northern French knights, under the leadership of Simon de Montfort (whose son began English democracy), acted as the military wing. Anyone who says that the barbaric massacres committed by Crusaders in Palestine meant that such warriors were uniquely anti-Islamic is proved wrong by de Montfort's capture of one Cathar town. He gave instructions to massacre *all* the inhabitants. When a fellow soldier chided him for killing the local Christians as well as the town's heretics, his blood-chilling reply was, "God will know his own," and the entire city was captured, then butchered. Crusaders were not just savage against Muslims and Jews but against fellow Europeans if they felt the need dictated.

In fact, one could say that all the Crusades succeeded except those in Palestine, and it is the latter's failure that makes that series of wars exceptional.

Spiritually, however, the Crusades of any description were a total disaster. Jesus used the power of the Holy Spirit and the faithful witness of ordinary Christians, often under dire persecution, to spread the good news of salvation. There were no sword-waving Christian troops to bring the gospel worldwide. Jesus made it clear that His weapons were not those of this world, and while it is true that the New Testament does employ martial language—referring to battles and Christian soldiers—it is more than obvious that these are spiritual metaphors, not actual weapons to be used in armed combat. This is indeed, as we saw earlier, one of the most significant differences between early Christian faith and that of the dawn of Islam.

So when we see Christians misusing the language of the Bible and taking up the sword, what they are in effect doing, I would argue, is using the means of *jihadist* Islam—military conquest—not that of biblical Christian faith. In effect, this would be Christians using Muslim methods against their Islamic political enemy.

This is why to me as a Protestant evangelical, for twenty-first-century Christians to condone the Crusades and their wanton barbarity is not to be boldly politically incorrect (as one book title would have us believe). Rather it is to reduce the faith of Jesus Christ and God's own method of spreading the gospel down to the very level of Islamic violence that the politically incorrect say they so abhor. Our weapons are spiritual, as Paul shows us in Ephesians, not mounted Frankish knights wading knee-deep in the blood of innocent Arab Christians as well as of Jews and Muslims, as happened in the capture of Jerusalem.

Not only that, but as the Reformers rediscovered, as we shall see throughout the next chapter, God's people here on earth are not a geographical unit—Christendom—but the body worldwide of those who believe and trust in Jesus Christ as their Savior and Lord. It is Muslims who divide the world geographically into two—the *Dar al Islam* or Realm of Islam and the *Dar al Harb* or Realm of War. We as Christians divide it not physically but spiritually, between Christians, who live all over the globe, and those who reject Christian faith, many of whom are white Westerners of European ancestry, living next door to us as well as far away.

Not only that but the Crusaders actually destroyed, in the Fourth Crusade in 1204, the one great military power that could have defended southeast Europe against the Islamic invasion that overwhelmed it from the fourteenth century onward. This Crusade was against the

Byzantine Empire, from which Catholic Europe finally split doctrinally in 1054 over the issues we saw in the last chapter. The Fourth Crusade was based upon pure greed—namely, that of the Italian city-states such as Venice to expand their commercial empires—and did nothing at all to combat Islamic control of the Middle East. Even by its own criteria, therefore, it was a failure. While the Byzantine—or East Roman—Empire was restored in 1261, it was now fatally weakened and would disappear altogether in 1453 when an Islamic power, the Ottoman Empire, conquered it by capturing the capital, Constantinople, turning it into the Istanbul we know today.

So the Crusades were not just against Muslims in the Middle East but against many other enemies. Politically they failed to keep Jerusalem, and spiritually they created a wholly false way of seeing the gospel. As we shall see in our final chapter, they also enabled present-day extremist Muslims to paint a completely wrong picture of Christianity, one that continues to harm the gospel in areas where Islam predominates now.

The Christendom mentality also caused another major spiritual setback, one not rectified until over a century or more after the Reformation began. This was the failure to bring the gospel to non-European peoples, and in particular the tragic missed opportunity to evangelize China centuries before the great missionary movement of the eighteenth century.

Even after the fall of Rome in 476, the church had continued to be very active evangelistically, bringing the gospel to the pagan Germans and Slavs, the latter being the major new inhabitants of Europe in what is now central and southeast Europe.

Although many groups converted at least nominally to Christianity—for example, the Angles and Saxons in England—evangelism beyond the borders of Europe did not happen. When North African Christianity fell to the Islamic invasions, a whole vast area that had been Christian for centuries effectively evaporated. Cross-cultural mission in such areas would in any case have been exceptionally difficult, as it still remains in Muslim countries today. But large groups were completely unevangelized in the east, where such barriers did not exist. One whole Turkic tribe, the Khazars, for example, actually converted to Judaism rather than to Christianity or Islam.

Some tenuous evangelism had happened in the east, however, and this was the effort of the Nestorian Christians to spread Christianity cross-culturally into what is now central Asia and China. Unfortunately, as we saw in the last chapter, Nestorians had many doctrinal quirks and views we would hold to be unorthodox. Nevertheless, unlike Western Christians, they did want to take the good news to peoples who had never heard it before.

At the end of the twelfth century a hitherto obscure Mongol nomad leader, Temujin, seized power over his tribe and began a series of conquests that would within a few years see the largest land-based empire on contiguous territory that has ever existed in history before or since. This was the Mongol Empire, which stretched at its peak from the Korean border on its east to the Polish on its west. In 1206 he proclaimed himself Great Khan with the name by which we now know him—Genghis (or Chinggis) Khan.

Genghis was a shaman, and most of the Mongols' leaders were too. But some of them were married to Nestorian wives, and when, for example, Hulagu Khan invaded what is now Iran in 1258 and destroyed the Muslim Abbasid caliphate's capital, Baghdad, he specifically decreed that Christians should be exempt from being massacred, at the request of his Nestorian wife. Similarly, the mother of Kublai Khan, the now legendary yet very real life ruler of China, was also a Nestorian believer.

One of the great legends of the Middle Ages was a mythical ruler called Prester John. This character almost certainly did not exist, but the legend of a great Christian ruler somewhere way beyond the borders of Europe was a powerful one throughout medieval times. It is possible that he was based upon the Christian kings of Ethiopia or upon stories of Nestorian-influenced rulers such as the Mongol Khans.

The Mongols, for a brief time between the 1250s and 1290s, saw the Christian West as an ally against Islam, although the West came close on many occasions to being invaded by the Mongols. Furthermore, if the centuries of Mongol rule over Russia are anything to go by, it is just as well that the West never succumbed to Mongol invasion and mayhem. But the Great Khan, Mongke, whose capital was in Karakorum in present-day Mongolia, was certainly interested in relations with the West through Nestorians at his court and with the Catholic Church in particular.

He therefore asked the Pope to send Catholic missionaries to his domains, thousands of miles away. Some brave priests did agree to go on what was then a very hazardous journey, the most famous missionary being William of Rubruck (c. 1215–1255), from what was then northern France on the orders of King Louis IX. His account still exists, and it is a sad saga of missed opportunities. Not only was he not particularly successful, but there was almost no follow-up to his mission. The Mongol rulers in Iran became Muslims—the Il-Khans—and the opportunities in that region thus disappeared, never to return. Some bold Franciscans did make the epic journey to China, and in 1278 there was briefly a Catholic bishop in Cambulac, the name we give for the city now called Peking or Beijing.

But few others went, and then came the Black Death, the dreadful bubonic plague that wiped out literally millions of people from China to Europe. The Great Schism, which we shall consider shortly, did not help either, and the successor in central Asia to the Mongols, Tamerlaine (or Timur-I-Leng), was a bloodthirsty ruler, a loyal Muslim, and no friend of Christianity. The pleas by Christians in China and Iran went unheeded, and not until the eighteenth century did Christian missionaries return to east Asia, this time with far happier results.

Christianity, in other words, stayed a sadly European-based faith, with just tiny remnants of what had been powerful Christian churches elsewhere in the Middle East.

One of the major legacies of North African Christianity remains with us, although now in the twenty-first century this phenomenon has begun a sharp decline. This is monasticism.

The notion of living cut off from the rest of the world, in isolation from it, was unknown to the early church and indeed contradicts Scripture since Christians are supposed to be salt and light in the communities in which God has placed them. While some groups, such as the Jewish Essenes, lived ascetic lives in the wilderness, as did John the Baptist, this was not at all the norm since Jesus and His disciples lived active lives within their communities. The apostle Paul, while clearly unmarried himself, made it plain that his was not the usual calling and that to be celibate was not at all to be superior.

Furthermore, the very idea of the body being inferior is not a biblical one at all but comes from Gnosticism, a teaching that, as we saw earlier, the apostles John and Paul condemned most vigorously in their epistles.

Historians differ as to when monasticism began, but most of them think it was around the fourth century, in northern Africa. Monasticism had been practiced in Asia for a long time—Buddhist monasteries date back for centuries, for example—and similar eastern imports include the halo around the heads of saints in pictures, which is also Buddhist in origin.

Initially the movement began with hermits living on their own in the desert. These include Anthony (256–356) and Simon Stylites (c. 390–456) who became famous for his unusual lifestyle of living on the top of a pillar.

Monasticism as we know it probably started around 320 with a community in the Egyptian desert founded by Pachomius, who lived about 290–346. This community became distinguished when the great Bible translator Jerome translated its rules into Latin. Bible memorization was compulsory to gain entrance, and anyone illiterate wishing to join was taught to read and write.

We must as Protestants be fair to some of monasticism's greatest achievements. The monks were careful to preserve the written Word of God, and we owe the survival of countless collections of Scripture to the monks who did so much to perpetuate them and protect them, especially in the West, from marauding pagan invaders.

When the barbarian invasions came at the end of the Roman Empire in the west (and those of Islam two centuries later), it was often the libraries of the great monasteries that helped preserve not just the Scriptures but Western civilization itself. This was especially so in Europe, as all other forms of knowledge, especially secular, had been utterly destroyed. The achievement of Martin of Tours (who died in 397) in bringing the monastic movement to the West is therefore historically very important, as monks preserved literacy at a time when the invaders were illiterate.

By 800 and the accession to the new Holy Roman Empire of its first ruler, Charlemagne, the preservation in monasteries of so much learning created a major outpouring of knowledge, usually described as the Carolingian Renaissance. Countless documents from Roman times were rediscovered, and it is more than likely that many monasteries had actually preserved the Latin originals, which were then copied en masse and distributed throughout the empire.

The Eastern Roman Empire, Byzantium, had never fallen, and a vast corpus of learning—medical, theological, and scientific—came to the West, often through the unusual route of Arabs who had picked up Greek knowledge, improved upon it, and then transmitted it on to the West. This was especially true of the major intellectual movement now called the Twelfth Century Renaissance, in which a huge body of literary, mathematical, philosophical, and medical knowledge, long discussed in places such as Baghdad or Cordoba, now reached eager recipients in the West. While we often think of the Middle Ages as being barbaric, such a view is in fact mistaken, as they knew a great deal more than we realized until recent times.

In the medieval West, by far the best known of the great monastic orders was that of St. Benedict, whose monks were called Benedictines. Anyone who has read or seen on television the series on an imaginary monk, *Brother Cadfael*, will be familiar with this order. We do not know a great deal about St. Benedict of Nursia (c. 480–c. 550—even his dates are uncertain), who died in what is now Italy, at Monte Cassino, scene of the epic battle fought there in World War II when a later monastery was destroyed. Benedict's own monastery was destroyed not long before his death, around 547. Rumor has it that he fled to Rome. There a monk named Gregory discovered Benedict's rule of how best to live an effective monastic life. This second monk later became Pope Gregory the Great, and it was he who made the Rule of St. Benedict famous. It is for all intents and purposes the rule on which most subsequent Catholic orders have based their monastic way of life ever since.

Life in a monastery centered on the works of God, or *opus dei* in Italian (this has nothing to do with the strange and very modern Catholic sect made notorious in *The Da Vinci Code*). In essence these included prayer, praise, Scripture reading, meditation, and often hard physical work. Every day was strictly regulated and divided into seven slots:

Lauds (*very* early morning prayer)
Prime (between Lauds and Terce)
Terce (around 9 A.M.)
Sext (noon)
None (3 P.M.)
Vespers (or evening prayers)
Compline (pre-bedtime prayers)

The person in charge of each monastery was the abbot, who looked after and directed the spiritual needs of the community. There was a tremendous amount of singing and also of copying out the Scriptures, all this long before the invention of printing. The monks performed all the chores, such as cleaning, gardening, and the making of meals. Every monk took a vow of poverty and celibacy and of lifelong obedience to the abbot.

Similar institutions existed for nuns, where an abbess played the role of abbot.

Scholarship was also at a premium in the monasteries, since their inhabitants were often the only people who could read and write. One of the earliest great scholars was Anselm (c. 1033–1109), a Norman monk who became Archbishop of Canterbury. Since philosophy in those days was a subset of theology, Anselm combined both disciplines. His major work was *Cur Deus Homo*, dealing with the question, why did God become man? Here he argued very much as we would now—namely, that God the Father forgives the sins of those who have faith in Jesus Christ because of what He accomplished for us on the cross.

Anselm also dealt with a very twenty-first-century issue, that of how we know that God exists at all. This is part of *ontology*. As Anselm put it in a phrase that became famous, *credo ut intelligam* (I believe in order that I may understand).

Anselm was also a firm believer in practical Christianity. He did all possible to abolish the slave trade—at that time, white people captured by other whites—and also never hesitated to stand up for what he believed to be the truth, even though that would entail strong disagreement with the king.

Unfortunately, much scholarship in time degenerated into obscurity and intellectual rigidity, known as Scholasticism. It has been parodied by the actual debate that raged on how many angels could dance upon the head of a single pin! Scholastics did not always agree with one another or with different groups or schools of opinion.

Two medieval scholastics remain well-known—Peter Abelard (1079–1142) and the even more famous Thomas Aquinas (c. 1225–1274), who remains one of the most important thinkers in the Roman Catholic Church to this very day.

Abelard is best known today for his illicit love affair with a French woman named Heloise. For this romance he was castrated and compelled to become a Benedictine monk. But philosophically he is distinguished for his treatise *Sic et Non* (*Yes and No*). Published in 1122, this was one of the more successful attempts in the Middle Ages to work out how faith and human reason can genuinely be reconciled, a major medieval concern. This work is significant. In discussing these two perennial topics, he sought to find out what the ultimate source of authority ought to be. Some think that he set off a chain of inquiry that would ultimately lead to the Reformation and the Protestant discovery that the Bible contains the ultimate source.

Aquinas, born in Italy, is regarded as by far the greatest of all the medieval scholastics, with an influence that stretches to the twenty-first century. A pupil of Abelard, his most famous work is his *Summa Theologica* ("summary of theology").

Aquinas was also keen to reconcile human reason and divine truth. While these debates may seem obscure to many today, they do have plenty of contemporary resonance. We as evangelicals in the twenty-first century are still wrestling with problems of applying our faith to contemporary culture, something, for example, to which Francis Schaeffer devoted much of his life in the twentieth century. So while much of what Aquinas wrote seems strange to us, the basic principles remain the same.

The thought of Aquinas is now called Thomism, and Roman Catholics have been obliged to follow it since 1879.

Besides the rise of monasticism, this period also saw the increasing power and influence of the Papacy. We saw that the post of Bishop of Rome was the great survivor of the fall of the Western Empire in the fifth century. The Pope still uses titles from imperial Rome, such as *Pontifex Maximus*, from which we get the English alternative name for Pope, Supreme Pontiff. But we also saw that, for example, at the Council of Constantinople in 381, five church leaders, or Patriarchs, were regarded as having great authority, and the Bishop of Rome was only one of them. But what is significant is that he was the only one representing the West, and after 476 western Europe was cut off from the rest of the Christian world.

However, we must be careful not to read back the universal claims of current Popes to many of their early predecessors—the growth of papal authority was a gradual process and one that was able to accelerate especially after Charlemagne reestablished a kind of Roman Empire in 800.

Having said that, earlier Popes such as Gregory did exert a wide authority, with that particular Pope, for example, being active in organizing the evangelism of England.

What, I think, made a huge difference were the Muslim invasions of the seventh century. This destroyed most of the remaining Patriarchates, those of Alexandria, Jerusalem, and Antioch, all of which were now under Islamic rule. Only Constantinople remained, and that was in effect not independent, being very much under the authority of the Byzantine emperor. This left just Rome, and as western Europe was in a state of major flux, only Rome remained independent, all the more so as the Pope was also now a secular ruler. This was the so-called Patrimony of St. Peter, the Papal States, a swath of territory in central Italy that the Popes ruled between then and 1870, of which the existence of the Vatican as an independent country is the last remnant today.

In theory after 800 the Pope wielded spiritual authority and the Holy Roman Emperor secular authority. But the Popes always insisted that the emperors ruled by papal grace and favor, and a medieval forgery, the so-called Donation of St. Peter, pretended to make this explicit. So whereas the Patriarch of Constantinople ruled by favor of the Byzantine emperor, the Popes insisted that the Holy Roman Emperor ruled by papal blessing. The situation in the West was the mirror image of that in the East, and the authority of the Popes correspondingly grew powerful.

We see the two very opposite ways in which this happened through two incidents, centuries apart.

In the Eastern Empire, Emperor Leo III realized in 726 that the icons in the Byzantine churches were not scriptural. In particular he was very influenced by the biblical account of King Josiah, who rid the Temple in Jerusalem of images and restored pure worship. Being emperor, Leo could do what he wanted, and all the icons were removed in a movement whose name still exists in a similar meaning: *iconoclasm*. But sixty years later the regent Theodora sacked the then Patriarch and in 787 insisted on reinstalling all the icons, whence they have remained in Eastern Orthodox churches ever since.

By contrast, in the eleventh century a powerful Christian prelate, Hildebrand, was elected Pope Gregory VII in 1073. Many of his reforms we would agree with fully, for like many of the much later reformers, he was well aware of the moral corruption that had entered the church, and he fought it furiously and effectively. But to do this he also had to reassert papal authority, since one of the major problems he encountered was secular (or lay) control over many ecclesiastical appointments. This seriously alienated him from the then Holy Roman Emperor, Henry IV, who wanted to exercise such control himself since bishops and abbots were now powerful landowners and secular rulers in the imperial heartland, Germany. Gregory thereupon excommunicated—expelled from the church—the emperor in 1077. As a result Henry IV was forced to wait barefoot in the freezing cold for several days outside the papal castle in Canossa, Italy until Pope Gregory condescended to allow him in and forgive his disobedience. More of a contrast between Rome and Constantinople could not be imagined, and as we have seen, in 1054 the two split permanently, theoretically over spiritual issues (*filioque*) but in practice over who was in overall control.

Unfortunately for the Papacy, many subsequent Popes were not of the mettle of Gregory VII. It is important for us as Protestants to remember that not all medieval Popes were corrupt or immoral like the Borgias and that some of them were godly. Not only that, but as we shall see with Francis of Assisi and followers of such movements as the *Devotio Moderna*, there were plenty of sincere believers, even though we might not agree with them on many other issues. I do not think we can hold to the view that God totally abandoned His Church for over a thousand years!

But politics did find its way back into the Papacy and on how Popes were chosen. This caused what is now known as the *Great Schism*, a period in the Middle Ages when there were two rival Popes, one in Rome and the other in Avignon in southern France (at one brief stage there were actually three Popes simultaneously). How did this happen?

In 1305 a Frenchman, Pope Clement V, was elected, and this increasingly took the Popes under French political domination and to a new base, Avignon. In 1381 two rival Popes were elected, one recognized in Rome, the other by the French at Avignon. Who supported whom was often entirely political. England disliked France and so supported the Pope in Rome, while Scotland, disliking England, supported the one in France.

Not until 1415, at the Council of Constance—at which Jan Hus was martyred—was unity restored in the person of Pope Martin V. All this greatly discredited the church. The schism helped to remove the sense of Catholic unity that had existed hitherto, something that was to prove important when the major changes of the Reformation took place in the sixteenth century.

However, as I mentioned before, it is vital to remember as Protestants that there were plenty of people in the Middle Ages who *did* want to stand for truth, even if they did not see it as clearly as we might want them to have done in retrospect. Luther did not spring out of the blue—plenty of reform and discussion had in fact been going on for centuries.

We will discuss Francis of Assisi and the great German Abbess Hildegard of Bingen shortly. All such people were, I feel, sincere reformers, even though none of them went as far as Luther and those in the sixteenth century would later. But I do think they had major achievements and acted well with the understanding that they had.

Others, such as the Englishman John Wycliffe (or Wycliff) and the Czech Jan Hus, went far further and in a spiritual sense saw things even more clearly. Since I want to argue in this book that the Reformation was well under way long before 1517, its traditional starting date, we will look at such people in the next chapter. But there were also some others who while not as theologically clear also realized there was much wrong with the church and in their own way tried to do something about it.

Some of these are called Christian mystics. The first of these was Julian of Norwich (1342–1413) who, despite her name, was a woman. In 1373 she had some powerful visions, putting them down on paper some twenty years later in a book still read today entitled *Sixteen Revelations of Divine Love.*

Julian had herself been much influenced by an anonymous medieval writer, the author of the still famous book *The Cloud of Unknowing*. This work made the important theological point, vital in the light of all the philosophical debates going on at the time, that we cannot get to know God through pure human reason alone. Only God can break through the barrier and reach out to us.

Contemporary with this was the German writer and mystic Meister (= Master) Eckhart, who lived around 1260–1327. Also still much read today, he was to prove a great influence on Luther's development and thinking two centuries later. A Dominican, he was also educated in France and lived in Bohemia, and his *Book of Divine Consolation* is fascinating for its powerful emphasis—later taken up by Luther—on the importance and centrality of faith. Unfortunately, many modern mystics also like him, but that should not detract us from what he actually wrote at the time.

However, we should not forget that the Middle Ages was a pre-dominantly illiterate age, a condition that remained, alas, even in much of the West right up until mass literacy and education in the nineteenth century.

As a consequence the church had to teach much truth visually. One version we as Protestants still use in evangelism, namely drama, at which we shall look later. The other one, which the Reformation rejected, was the cult of saints and the existence of many statues in churches and shrines to those saints.

The Medieval Sacraments

The Reformation, as we shall see, abolished most of the sacraments of the Roman Catholic Church. So as Protestants we need to be reminded of those practices, or sacraments, which were so important in medieval times and which many Catholics still maintain today.

By the thirteenth century, and especially the Fourth Lateran Council of 1215, the church regarded seven sacraments as being of special importance. These were: baptism, confirmation, Eucharist (= Holy Communion), penance/confession, extreme unction (a special blessing on those about to die), ordination, and marriage.

The notion behind the sacraments is that they are the outward signs of the grace that God gives, which is normally His inward work in our lives. The Catholic Church regarded them as having been begun by Christ Himself, an idea that the Reformation rejected. The Catholic Church still teaches that these sacraments in and of themselves can confer God's grace upon an individual, again a notion that the Reformation refuted.

Hagiolatry, the worship of saints, is not limited to Catholicism—the Sufi, or mystic branch, of Islam, similarly worships saints, or *pirs*. Furthermore, I think we can say this is the *result* of a spiritual problem rather than the cause of it. Scripture teaches that we can approach God directly in prayer, through the Holy Spirit, as a result of Christ's finished work upon the cross. Saint worship is the outcome of false teaching that we need especially holy intermediaries to intercede between God and us. We as Protestants ought also to remember the parable of the speck and the log—how often have we asked fellow Christians whom we think to be particularly godly to pray for us, in the hope that their prayers are more likely to be answered? But each of us has spiritual flaws or shortcomings. How much, too, do we indulge in the cult of evangelical substitute saints? Is it Scripture that determines our doctrine, or St. Calvin or St. Spurgeon? Before we rise in wrath at past malpractice, we ought carefully to consider how guilty we are, even if our form of hagiolatry is different.

Strictly and biblically speaking, all Christians are saints—"the saints in Ephesus" and similar phrases in the New Testament epistles come to mind. But over the course of time some Christians seem to have been revered more than others, and as I have just argued, it is a natural human tendency to desire heroes, people whom we admire so much that we put them on a pedestal. Unfortunately, the original biblical criteria for sainthood—simply a word synonymous with being a Christian—was altered to fit only those given special awe and reverence. As the biblical doctrine of direct access through the Holy Spirit to God was forgotten, saints became popular as substitute intermediaries, especially if they came from your own locale, color group, or ethnicity. Nations, craft guilds, and many other groups ended up with special patron saints of their own, to whom special favors could be addressed—England with St. George, doctors with St. Luke, and so on.

We cannot see God, and as Jesus tells Thomas, those of us who believe without seeing are blessed precisely because we have faith in Christ *without* ever having seen Him with our own eyes. As the author of Hebrews reminds us, faith is the substance of things *not seen*.

But, alas, people always prefer what they *can* see, and it is all too easy to understand how the images of saints, and of Christ Himself, came to be substituted for true faith as time went by. As my old Classics master once shrewdly observed, patron saints are in many ways a substitute for the household deities, or *lares et penates*, of ancient Rome. While the novel *The Mists of Avalon*, set in Arthurian England, has much wrong with it theologically, its own pagan heroine's observation that the cult of the Virgin Mary was a substitute for the pagan worship of the Mother Goddess, while not necessarily always accurate, has a lot going for it as an explanation.

In addition, ordinary people felt that the saints were more approachable. Look too at many Virgin and Child pictures—Christ is always far smaller than His mother, and she often has a degree of empathy that is designed to make her the best means of approaching Jesus, her Son. Mary was, in the Orthodox world, called the Mother of God, which is, of course, a theological impossibility. Mariolatry in the Catholic Church has in fact evolved over centuries, and one can argue that it was not until the twentieth century that much of the false teaching about her became the official dogma of the Roman Catholic Church, as comparatively recently as 1950.

Recent writers, most notably Eamon Duffy, have pointed out that pre-Luther parish life was not quite perhaps as dire as we have imagined. We shall also see that Duffy is right to say that folk Catholicism lasted much longer in England, and maybe elsewhere, than Protestants like to think—the survival of the Reformation in England was much narrower than we realize.

Parish life is not always easy to reconstruct because of the paucity of written materials, many of which were, in any case, destroyed by the Reformers in the sixteenth century.

But we obtain a clear picture from liturgical books for educated laypeople—items such as *Books of Hours* or primers—fifty thousand of which have survived to our own time. So while the leadership may often have been corrupt, that was not at all true of the grass roots. For the mass of uneducated people, the church had "mystery plays," based upon biblical themes and the lives of popular saints. One of these "cycles" (often acted out on festival or other special days), is the York Mysteries. So we can know what people saw then.

If you visit England, you will see that many churches built in medieval times have side chapels or chantries—in Italy these buildings were sometimes large enough to be freestanding chapels in their own right. These were nearly all commissioned by laypeople, usually wealthy businessmen, so the clergy of a particular parish could say prayers for the soul of the deceased donor. While we reject the doctrine of purgatory (as many moderate Catholics also do today), the existence of all the chantries does show a strong lay activity within the church. So too does the existence of numerous craft guilds for skilled craftsmen, many of whom also endowed churches and had chantries of their own.

Lay involvement, as we shall soon see, was one of the keys to the Protestant Reformation of the sixteenth century—indeed, humanly speaking without it Luther would never have survived at all, let alone have the spiritual impact that he did. All this goes to prove, I would argue, that there were genuinely seeking people long before we have traditionally expected and that well over a century before the great events of what we call the Reformation the seeds were sown for what Luther and the others accomplished. Not only that, but many of the forerunners were not famous like Hus or Wycliffe but were unknown, God-seeking businessmen and their families who yearned to know God, experience Christ, and be familiar with God's Word.

Francis of Assisi

Francis of Assisi (c. 1181–1226), known to Catholics as St. Francis, was one of the giants of the Middle Ages. The order he founded in 1208—the Franciscans—still exists and also has a Protestant wing, Third Order Franciscans.

Francis was born to a wealthy background in the Italian town of Assisi. But in 1208 he felt a strong calling from God to give up his life of privilege and follow Jesus, based upon Matthew 10:7-19. Based upon this, he and his followers began living lives of absolute simplicity, and in 1210 the Pope, Innocent III, gave the new order official sanction.

This new group was called the Friars Minor, and in 1212 a similar group was founded for women, the Poor Clares. The two orders were deliberately evangelistic from the start and were able to gain enormous credence among ordinary people since their sincerity and simplicity was obvious to all, unlike that of much of the corrupt institutional church.

This was, needless to say, a threat to the clerical establishment, and Pope Honorius III did his best to rein in the new order. Francis himself was no administrator and retired to a small hermitage, where he died in 1226. The church liked the good image he gave them, however, and he was canonized with unusual rapidity only two years after his death, in 1228.

Sadly, but perhaps not surprisingly, the original simplicity did not long outlive its founder. The "Spirituals" among his followers wanted to keep to the original rule of no property, while the others were quite happy to take land and money for monasteries and the like. In 1317 the more spiritually minded set up their own independent order, the Fraticelli. It is from those who did accept gifts that today's Franciscans descend.

Many famous medieval thinkers were Franciscans. This includes the great British thinker William of Ockham (or Occam; c. 1285–1347), from whom we gain the expression Occam's Razor (the simplest solution to a problem is usually the right one).

Franciscans, who have the initials OFM (*Ordo Fratrum Minorum*; Order of Friars Minor) after their name, are still influential today and now exist worldwide. In the twentieth century some at their university in Steubenville, Ohio had close links with evangelical groups in Michigan.

The "Prayer of St. Francis" is still widely known and used:

> Lord, make me an instrument of thy peace.
> Where there is hatred, let me sow love;
> Where there is injury, pardon;
> Where there is doubt, faith;
> Where there is despair, hope;
> Where there is darkness, light;
> Where there is sadness, joy.
>
> O Divine Master, grant that
> I may not so much seek to be consoled as to console;
> Not so much to be understood as to understand;
> Not so much to be loved as to love;
> For it is in giving that we receive;
> It is in pardoning that we are pardoned;
> It is in dying that we awaken to eternal life.

Hildegard of Bingen

The great Abbess Hildegard of Bingen (1098–1179), from Rupertsburg in what is now Germany, was one of the greatest women of medieval times and a good example of how influential a woman could be in those days.

Her music—she was a prolific composer—has become very popular again in recent years, and her work is now bought all over the world on CD. While some New Age people have taken her up, this does not in any way reflect her own theology, which was mainstream for its day. Those with migraines might well see her supposed visions of many colors in a medical, not mystic light. She was also a distinguished scientist and a great correspondent, especially with the Holy Roman

Emperor of the time, the great Frederick Barbarossa. She was an aristocrat and an intellectual and a good example of how a woman can play a significant role in church life (not to mention in culture and politics) in a way that does not usurp the role of men. The eighteenth-century Selina, Countess of Huntingdon, Whitefield's supporter, will be another example that we shall encounter later.

F O U R

The Reformation—
Martin Luther

God will purify [His] Holy Church by awakening the spirit of the elect.
This will lead to such an improvement in the Church of God and such
a renewal in the lives of her holy pastors that at the mere thought of it
my spirit exalts in the Lord.

Can you guess who wrote this?

Was the author of this piece John Calvin or perhaps Jan Hus or
John Wycliffe? In fact the answer is the "Catholic" writer Catherine
of Siena, who lived around 1347–1380.

In looking at the Reformation, I will mainly concentrate on what
happened and why. But before we go on to the exciting main narrative
itself, there are some theological issues that we need to deal with, and
then we will take a long look at the greatest figure of the Reformation,
Martin Luther.

Did the Reformation begin as a bolt out of the blue when Martin
Luther nailed his Ninety-five Theses to a church door in Wittenberg in
what is now Germany? Or, as I will argue here, had God in fact been

speaking for a long time to people seeking Him and thereby creating an environment in which the Reformation, when it finally came in full flow after 1517, was able to survive and thrive?

Put another way, do we believe that no one went to heaven from, say, the fourth century to the sixteenth? Must we say there were no genuine Christians in that whole 1,200-year period? Obviously, as an evangelical I would want to say that some who were converted in this period had theological flaws and held to doctrines that we now reject. But with no alternatives at that time, unlike today, it is surely hard to believe that apart from a few proto-Protestants, such as the Waldensians in Italy or the followers of Jan Hus and John Wycliffe, no one was saved at all. To put it another way, can we as evangelicals say that our loving Heavenly Father abandoned His church for over a millennium? Theologically that seems unlikely to me. Many Christians in that long period may not have seen things as clearly as we would now wish them to have done. But I do believe that their faith in Jesus Christ as their Lord and Savior was real despite having no vernacular Bible or the ability to read. God uses whatever means are available to bring people to faith.

I think the words of Catherine of Siena show that God was at work, speaking to people earnestly seeking Him, preparing the ground for the major return to biblical doctrine and practice that we now call the Reformation.

Second, how much of what I am writing here differs from books that you might have read in school or university? Is there a particularly evangelical way of writing about these epochal events?

In much of what follows I disagree strongly with secular writers on the great Reformers. Not only that, but as an evangelical with strongly Reformed views, I have a slant that would not be true, say, of a Roman Catholic writing on this subject. I do not, for example, think that the Reformation was a shame—a view held strongly by Catholic writers and by some liberal Protestants—except in that it was necessary because the church had gone so astray doctrinally and for so long a period.

However, in some areas I can see where such secular/Catholic historians are coming from. This is not in a spiritual sense—I attribute the Reformation to the work of the Holy Spirit in a way in which they do not. But I do think that God in His sovereignty used many secular and seemingly unrelated events to create a climate of opinion in which men like Luther could thrive. And, second, I feel that God inspired inventions such as the printing press and causes such as German nationalism that, though entirely secular, did help the cause of the gospel in the sixteenth century and beyond.

To secular historians, these are the main causes of the Reformation. To me they are all secondary to the main reason—the work of God. But there is no doubt that in the same way in which God used Cyrus or the Roman Empire to help His people spread the gospel, He also used man-made things for spiritual good ends. So while the secular historians are wrong to leave out the work of the Holy Spirit—admittedly, rather a major omission from a Christian standpoint—they are not totally wrong when they attribute much importance to what we would see as secular events. Our difference, as Christians, is not so much in whether or not these things—such as the printing press—helped but in attributing divine guidance to the difference that they made.

Third, although all of us as evangelicals think we agree on the Reformation, there are in fact major areas upon which we disagree with one another. This inevitably colors how we see these great events.

For example, during much of the Reformation Baptists were put to death, quite often *by fellow Protestant believers*. So it goes without saying that a Baptist and a Presbyterian would have very different perspectives on many of the doctrinal debates that took place as the Reformation unfolded. Not only that, but we forget that the Reformers took a long time to realize that state power should not be used coercively in Christian doctrinal disputes. (This is, I think, a discovery that is perhaps one of America's greatest contributions to Christianity.)

Consequently, one group of Christians would not hesitate to use the state to put to death those with whom they disagreed. We might have disagreements on such issues today, but to use the death penalty to enforce them is, I hope, completely beyond consideration! But that was not the case then, and the very existence of the USA today is to no small extent due to the desire of Christians to flee *fellow Protestants* and express their Christian faith as they felt the Bible dictated.

We must remember this in what we are about to read. We are right to make the founders of Protestantism into heroes, but we must also remember that they were human like us.

There is one final thing to recall. When the Reformation began, many saw it as a splitting of Christendom, the name given to the professing Christian western and central Europe. In terms of that part of the world, it is true that the Reformation divided it in two, and did so permanently. But we should not forget that the original split was made as long before as 1054, when the Catholic West and Orthodox East went their different doctrinal ways. That split still exists, and even in the early twenty-first century Orthodox countries such as Greece still persecute both Protestants and Catholics. Not only that, but because of the Islamic conquests of the fourteenth century onward, much of this latter part of the world was under Muslim rule until the twentieth century. There was no Reformation, let alone a Renaissance, in the Orthodox lands.

Early Reformers

Since I have argued that the Reformation was a process, we can now start to look at some of its great precursors, men like John Wycliffe (or Wycliff), who lived in England from 1324–1384 and was for a brief while Vice-Master of Balliol College, Oxford.

Wycliffe never started a new church. But like many of his contemporaries, he realized that the medieval church was going seriously astray. In his case he saw the decadence and corruption of much of the clergy, some of whom were more politicians or major landowners than priests and had mistresses and illegitimate children.

In 1377 Wycliffe got into trouble with the church authorities. Here he was fortunate: he had a political protector in John of Gaunt, a younger son of King Edward III (and the ancestor of today's British Royal Family). This was crucial since otherwise Wycliffe would have been executed, as Jan Hus would later be. John of Gaunt was no saint, but he did admire Wycliffe, and, as earlier in history, God used an unrighteous man to protect a godly one.

But what is crucial about Wycliffe is that he went on from realizing the obvious point about clergy corruption and saw several key doctrinal truths that we as Protestants now take for granted but were seen as revolutionary at that time.

First, he saw that in the Eucharist—the Lord's Supper—Christ was *spiritually* present but not, as the Catholic Church still teaches, *physically* present.

Second, and even more radical for the time, he realized that as the true church consisted of God's people, there was no need for a vast priestly hierarchy to mediate between the believers and God. Christians could relate directly to God themselves.

Third, he translated the Bible into English and in a way that ordinary people could read it for themselves. He is thus the ancestor of the numerous Bible translations that have appeared in the centuries since, down to the *English Standard Version* of our own day.

All this drastically undermined the position of the church as the mediator between God and the laity. Thanks to his political protection, Wycliffe was lucky to escape with his life intact, though he did have to leave Oxford University. He was able to retire to the countryside and die peacefully.

He managed to win many over to his cause. In time these followers were nicknamed Lollards, and the Catholic hierarchy did all it could to suppress them. One interesting reflection is that those areas in which many Lollards lived in the fourteenth century were often the most Protestant when the Reformation came two centuries later.

Jan Hus (1372–1415) was a Czech living in what was then called Bohemia, part of the Holy Roman Empire that existed from

A.D. 800–1806. He taught at the great European intellectual center, the Charles University in Prague, and preached at the Bethlehem Chapel nearby, a place that still exists.

Hus was deeply influenced by Wycliffe. Unlike most of their contemporaries, who believed that being born in a Christian country made you a Christian—the idea of Christendom—Hus, like Wycliffe, knew that only true believers constituted the church. Only God, he taught, not priests, could forgive sins.

Even more radically, he taught that Scripture rather than the teaching of the church was the sole source of authority—the doctrine the later Reformers would call *sola scriptura*, or Scripture alone. This view and his robust condemnation of both clergy corruption and popular superstition made him deeply unpopular with the church hierarchy.

As a result he was summoned to appear at the Council of Constance in 1415. This was the Council that ended the decades of Catholic division—the Great Schism. But though the Holy Roman Emperor had provided Hus with safe conduct, the church authorities ignored that and burned him to death at the stake. Hus became a martyr and also a Bohemian national hero, something he was to remain even under Communist rule in Czechoslovakia in 1948–1989. The Hussite Church thrived until its suppression in 1620 and, in a much attenuated form, still exists today.

Hus and Wycliffe were doctrinal radicals whose theological views went well beyond the need to deal with political corruption and moral decadence within the church. They did not set up a new church as such, although their followers operated outside of the Catholic umbrella. There were those, however, who while realizing that the rot had set in—the flagrant immorality of the Borgia Pope Alexander being a prime example—nonetheless felt they should stay within the church in an attempt to reform it internally.

By far the best example of such godly reformers were Christians in what is now the Netherlands—then also part of the Holy Roman Empire—who followed what was called the *Devotio Moderna* ("modern devotion"). Their founder was Geert de Groote (1340–1384), a preacher with a strong emphasis on personal holiness. But they are best known for their followers.

The first of these was Florens Radewijns (1350–1400), who founded an even more famous community, the Brethren of the Common Life. Their most distinguished member was Thomas à Kempis (1380–1471), the author of the great classic *The Imitation of Christ*. This is probably one of the most famous medieval devotional books and remains in print to this day. It is deliberately Christ-centered and calls upon us to follow Christ whatever the cost to ourselves.

The other person deeply influenced by the Brethren of the Common Life was Erasmus of Rotterdam (1466–1536). It is said of Erasmus that he laid the egg for the Reformation and Luther hatched it. His book *In Praise of Folly*, written not far from where the *English Standard Version* of the Bible was translated in Cambridge, England, was a devastating critique of all that had gone wrong with the medieval church. Overall his work was able to make an enormous intellectual contribution in Europe that in turn led many people to realize that the church urgently needed reforming.

Erasmus also produced a much-improved Greek translation of the Bible, which was also to be of much use when the Reformation came.

Erasmus was an internal critic of the church. He knew its many faults, but it never occurred to him to try to re-create the church that had existed in the beginning. But he saw what had gone wrong, for example, with the Papacy. As Pope Leo X, a member of the Medici dynasty, said on being elected Pope, "Now that we have attained the papacy, let us enjoy it!"

So we can see a process here—from Catherine of Siena, to Wycliffe and Hus, to the Brethren of the Common Life and Erasmus, right down to the actual dawn of the Reformation itself in 1517. Over the course of two centuries God was clearly speaking to devout Christians who sought Him and who were doing their utmost to lead godly lives as best as they knew how.

Luther's Story

In 1517, in an obscure, intellectually backward part of the Holy Roman Empire from which no one ever expected anything much in the way of innovation, an event took place that sparked what we now call the Protestant Reformation.

However, that is how we see it in retrospect—at the time no one could possibly have predicted that what began as an academic debate would have permanent, earth-shattering, spiritual consequences.

It began in the form of a discussion—the Ninety-five Theses or arguments that a young monk, Martin Luther, pinned to the door of a church in Wittenberg in the Electorate of Saxony on October 31, 1517.

The Catholic Church taught that in between death and heaven exists a place called purgatory. As its name implies, it was a limbo existence, and the teaching of indulgences claimed that if you gave a donation or committed a spiritually meritorious deed, the Pope had the power to shorten the time that your loved ones had to spend there. In other words, a cash donation could speed up heaven.

The reason for the need for money was so the Archbishop Elector of Mainz, who was also a young German prince, could pay off some of his financial obligations.

Interestingly enough, while writing this book I read in the Catholic journal *The Tablet* that the church still believes fully in indulgences, although the cash element is no longer part of it.

All this outraged Luther. This is why as a university professor he decided to start an academic debate on these practices. But by 1520 what had begun as a simple discussion had developed into such a major threat to the authority of the Catholic Church that Luther was excommunicated by no less than the Pope himself.

Specifically Luther was protesting the sale of indulgences by a priest named Tetzel. Who was Martin Luther?

Luther (1483–1546) was the son of a prosperous copper miner from Saxony, in what is now eastern Germany. Saxony was not exactly the center of the intellectual universe, although it was not a backwater either. But it was certainly outside the cultural and political mainstream of early modern Europe, and no one would have predicted that someone from there, and from what we would now call a skilled working class family, would produce the seismic spiritual revolution to which we give the name the Reformation.

I have written much more about Luther elsewhere. So this, alas, will have to be a key summary of his life. Luther was originally destined to be a lawyer, and had he become one, he would have been superb at it—he argued with consummate ease—but he would also in all likelihood have been forgotten by history.

But as a young man he was caught in a frightening thunderstorm. Crying out to St. Anne for help, he told God that if his life were spared he would become a monk. He survived, kept his promise, and became an Augustinian monk.

He was soon lecturing at the University in Wittenberg, a new institution founded by the Elector of Saxony. He was asked to teach a series on the book of Romans, and this would change not only his own life but those of countless millions since, leading first to the Ninety-five Theses and thence to the Reformation. What he found in that epistle is best delivered in his own words.

> I greatly longed to understand Paul's Epistle to the Romans, and nothing stood in the way but that one expression, "the righteousness of God," because I took it to mean that righteousness whereby God is righteous and deals righteously with punishing the unrighteous.
>
> Night and day I pondered it until . . . I grasped the truth that the righteousness of God is that righteousness whereby, through grace and sheer mercy, he justifies us by faith. Thereupon I felt myself to be reborn and to have gone through open doors to paradise. The whole of Scripture took on a new meaning, and, whereas before the expression the "righteousness of God" had filled me with hate, now it became to me inexpressibly sweet in greater love. This passage of Paul became to me a gateway to heaven.

Today it is all too easy as evangelical Protestants to take the availability of God's glorious grace for granted. But imagine if it were taught almost nowhere and you discovered it! This is how exciting and wonderful it was for Luther to rediscover the biblical doctrine that the righteous shall live by faith through the grace of God.

We have here the other great pillar of Reformation belief to add to *sola scriptura*, which is *sola fidei*, by faith alone. Again, as historians such as Alister McGrath and Euan Cameron remind us, we forget the revolutionary nature of this doctrine, one that entirely overthrew the carefully crafted Catholic structure of life with its countless rituals and rules, all of which had gone on for centuries. Now that the believer could relate *directly* to God, the power of the church as intermediary had gone.

This was also because it is by faith, not by works, that we are saved. The Catholic Church brimmed with good works that people could perform to merit their salvation, but Luther, by returning to the Bible, to salvation *by faith alone*, overturned this vast edifice completely.

Take too the phrase *born again*. It reminds many today of the book by former Nixon aide and Watergate prisoner Chuck Colson. It is, of course, an entirely biblical phrase, uttered by Jesus to the Pharisee, Nicodemus. There our Lord makes plain that unless someone is born again, he or she cannot enter the Kingdom of God. Therefore, *all* Christians are by definition born again. This was what Luther came to realize, and we fail to make it central at our peril.

Luther's 95 Theses

I will highlight some of these because they are so important a way of demonstrating the theological origins of the Reformation.

Protestantism comes from *protest*, as the movement began when Luther protested the clear abuses that had been going on for centuries. Protestants were not the only ones angry at the abuses—we have seen how against them Erasmus was, and the same could be said for Calvin's frequent correspondent (and Luther's almost exact contemporary) Gasparo Contarini (1483–1542), who was no less than a Cardinal himself. The main difference is that in what followed, Luther swiftly found himself on a trajectory that took him out of the Catholic Church and thus into founding something new.

What Luther was doing in his theses was to resurrect the biblical concept that, ironically in the light of Catholic teaching on the Papacy, is found in Peter's second epistle. This is *the priesthood of all believers*, namely that no separate caste of priests exists.

We see this in some of the theses. The other two doctrines, on Scripture and faith, are equally clear:

1. When our Lord Jesus Christ said "repent" . . . he meant that the whole life of believers should be one of repentance.
6. The Pope can remit no guilt, but only declare and confirm that it has been remitted by God.
27. There is no divine authority for preaching that the soul flies out of purgatory as soon as the money clinks in the collecting box.

Luther had not intended to start a return to a biblical form of church. But this is what happened because being excommunicated he was no longer able to reform the church from within. So in one sense one could say that it was a Pope who began the Reformation, by expelling Luther!

As we saw, God used secular events in an amazing way during this period, and few inventions could have been as gloriously timed as the Western invention of the printing press (the Chinese had been printing for centuries). For Luther, being an academic, his first thought was to write a series of pamphlets to take the debate further. Whereas in the past a few parchments might have reached a tiny handful of scholars, the invention of the printing press meant that tens of thousands of literate people were now able to read Luther's revolutionary views for themselves, and with dramatic results.

These pamphlets included *The Address to the Christian Nobility of the German Nation*, *The Babylonian Captivity of the Church*, and *The Freedom of the Christian Man*.

The first pamphlet shows the importance of the key role played by the German rulers in the survival of Protestantism. We saw that it was John of Gaunt who kept Wycliffe from being martyred and that Jan Hus's career as a reformer ended early at the stake. The latter would very likely have been Luther's fate also if he had not had a political protector, the Elector of Saxony, his local ruler. This in itself was far from inevitable since the Elector Frederick the Wise's main claim to fame locally was his enormous collection of sacred relics.

Luther's pamphlets had an enormous impact. So too did the woodcuts, an example of art playing a major role in shaping history. Many poor people were illiterate, but they could understand the message of a printed woodcut. Consequently a propaganda war now began, with Catholics portraying Luther and his followers as evil, and a growing number of Lutherans similarly caricaturing their Catholic enemies. From very early on it was impossible not to know about the major theological issues, and the debate was joined for the first time, from the most learned scholar to the most illiterate swineherd.

As a result, the emperor felt it necessary to be involved. But here too one can argue that God was at work in mysterious ways, using the unrighteous to help the godly.

Few rulers in history had the power of Emperor Charles V since he was ruler of more parts of Europe than any single person since Roman times. (Since he split his domains upon his abdication, no one until Napoleon over 250 years later had such power again.) He could in theory have strangled the infant Protestant movement at birth and swatted any pro-Luther princes like flies.

But the very size of his empire was a problem. Since he was also King of Spain and Archduke of Austria, his domain was threatened both from the south and from the north by the growing power of Islam, the Ottoman Empire. As a result his resources were massively overstretched, and the amount of time he could devote to crushing

Protestants was very small. It is an irony to which secular historians have only just awakened that it was the Islamic threat to Europe in the Mediterranean and in the Balkans that prevented Charles V from destroying the Protestant Reformation.

The main result was that for most of the time Charles was forced to parley and compromise with his slowly growing number of Protestant princes rather than wiping them out. We see this at the meeting of all the princes (which we should remember included Catholic clergy, such as the three Archbishops or Ecclesiastical Electors), called the Imperial Diet, in the city of Worms in 1521.

Not all historians agree that Luther used the precise words now attributed to him at the Diet of Worms when he was summoned to explain himself to the assembled rulers. Either way, though, I am sure that the gist of the words he supposedly used is true:

> Your Imperial Majesty and your Lordships demand a simple answer. Here it is plain and unvarnished. Unless I am convicted of error by the testimony of Scripture or—since I put no trust in the unsupported authority of Pope or [Church] Councils, since it is plain that they have often erred and often contradicted themselves—or by manifest reasoning, I stand convicted by the Scriptures to which I have appealed, and to act against our conscience is neither safe for us nor open to us. On this I take my stand. I can do no other. God help me! Amen.

The last phrases have rung down the centuries as the mighty clarion call of Protestant Christianity. But I have quoted what went before as it is essential to understand the context. Luther was overthrowing completely the entire edifice of papal authority and, since this was backed to the hilt by secular force, its political edifice as well. The Pope had no authority, and even the assembled might of the secular and ecclesiastical princes of the Empire had no right to enforce what was not true.

Again, we have here one of the key doctrines of the Reformation— *sola scriptura*, the authority of Scripture alone. This is at the heart of Protestantism and must surely be at the core of Evangelicalism today.

What is true, and how do we know what is true? The answer, always, must be not our feelings or what our favorite preacher says or what some best-selling book tells us but *what Scripture teaches*—Scripture, as Luther put it in his usual forthright way, "plain and unvarnished."

This doctrine is, I feel, a truth that we neglect at our peril and continues to be one of the key lessons of the Reformation for Christians in the twenty-first century and beyond. Even as I was writing this chapter, I heard confirmation from a worried pastor of what was once a mighty evangelical organization that is becoming more than confused not only at the edges but at the center. It is sadly no coincidence that the decline in the centrality of Scripture is at the heart of that ministry's tragic decay. We may not make the Pope a rival for authority as Protestants, but I am sure that we can all think of papal substitutes that have replaced the Bible as the source of truth for all too many professing Christians today.

Luther, meanwhile, having been excommunicated already by the Church, was now outlawed by the emperor. This put his life in immediate jeopardy and made martyrdom all the more likely. So on his way back from Worms he was "kidnapped," though not in the conventional way at all. Rather, the Elector of Saxony and his growing number of sympathizers knew that as Luther's life was in danger, he had to be conveyed to safety as soon as possible. The apparent kidnappers were in fact henchmen of the Elector, and Luther was incarcerated entirely for his own protection at the electoral castle of Wartburg. Here he was able to live, write, and think in peace, under the pseudonym of Knight George (*Ritter Georg*). From his new home came the inspiration for his famous hymn, "A Mighty Fortress Is Our God."

Here, ironically under protective lock and key, he wrote another of his famous pamphlets in 1525—*The Bondage of the Will*—a ringing declaration of Christian freedom.

But while Luther's time in Wartburg kept him safe from the emperor, his safety at the hands of the Elector was, we would now argue, two-edged in its consequences.

For Luther, the secular/sacred divide was literally doubled-edged—what one can call the *two swords theory*—the sword of the state and that of the church. This meant that it was legitimate to use the powers of the state on behalf of the church. This appealed to secular rulers since they could in effect control the church within their own borders. No longer would there be a Pope hundreds of miles away in Rome telling them what they could and could not do with church appointments and the vastly wealthy church lands situated within each ruler's territory. In many ways the latter was even more important as many Protestant princes seized church lands for themselves, greatly increasing their own revenues and powers and also accumulating plenty of land with which to reward their own nobility, as we shall see when we look at the Reformation in England.

In fact, the issue of patronage, linked closely with that of land, was one of the main reasons why so many secular princes and local free city councils opted for the Reformation, as Euan Cameron's book *The European Reformation* makes clear. This may not seem at all godly to us, and there were, thankfully, plenty of princes, knights, and city councillors whose spiritual conversion was surely very genuine. But as we will see in depth when looking at the English Reformation, a ruler's lust for power, for an heir to the throne, and for running his own show all added up to furthering the work of God in England in the long term.

Unfortunately for Luther and the princes in Germany, many ordinary readers of Luther's books equated the spiritual freedom they now enjoyed as Christians with the demand that they now wanted to have far more political freedom from their despotic local overlords. Thousands of peasants revolted, wishing no more than the liberties that we take for granted today.

Here Luther showed that he was all too much a man of his time. He sided with the princes against their own people. His next pamphlet was entitled *Against the Murdering and Thieving Hordes of Peasants*, and it made his views exceedingly clear. Catholic and Protestant dukes, knights, and princes suppressed the rebels. To Luther, the "voices of Satan," of the peasants, had to be crushed, so that good government—that of the princes—could be continued.

Luther's stand horrified followers in his own time. Herman Muehlporft did not hesitate to point out that the princes in their wrath were slaughtering many innocent women and children, which was, alas, the case.

Many princes did well because of the Reformation. We see this especially in England, where King Henry VIII pillaged church lands ruthlessly. Some of it he kept himself, and other portions of land he gave to faithful retainers, in effect to buy their loyalty. Take Woburn Abbey, for example, the home for nearly five hundred years of the Russell family, the Dukes of Bedford. Go around some of the buildings, and it is possible actually to see where the cloisters were originally situated. Many an aristocratic family in Britain owes its ancestral wealth to the dissolution of the monasteries in the 1530s.

Long-term this had an interesting effect of helping the nobility support Protestantism: if the Catholics ever regained power, there was always the danger that the restored church would demand the return of the pillaged lands.

It was similar, albeit on a smaller scale, in other parts of Europe as well. Kings and princes discovered that they could exercise political control over their local clergy, who could not, in a Protestant state, appeal to Rome for help. No longer could some proud king such as Henry VIII be denied his wishes by a Pope hundreds of miles away and outside of his control.

Luther, we must remember, did not set out to create a new form of Christian church—it was imposed upon him by outside events. This is important—we cannot accuse Luther, as Catholics have done, of splitting Christianity since it was papal reaction, and that of Catholic princes in Germany, especially the Emperor Charles V, that actually did the splitting by the way in which they treated Luther. Having said that, a split would inevitably have come sooner or later since it was obvious to increasing numbers of godly people that what was wrong with the Catholic Church was more than cosmetic, but actually something doctrinally and fundamentally wrong.

Without the thought processes through which Luther traveled, the Reformation would not have been possible. For while Erasmus and similar folk knew what had gone wrong with the Roman Catholic Church, they had stayed within it. Through understanding what *the Bible itself* actually taught, Luther realized that cosmetic changes to the Catholic Church would not be enough—what was required was something infinitely more drastic and fundamental.

The Catholic Reaction

Eventually the Catholic hierarchy and princely supporters realized that Protestantism was there to stay and could not be crushed, militarily or otherwise.

Historically this has been known as the *Counter-Reformation*. Historians now like to see the whole process as one of continual change and use the word *Reformation* to cover both the origins and development of Protestantism, as well as the reaction to it by the Catholic Church. To some extent this is a semantic argument, but there is a point to it because without the rise of Protestantism it is possible that no internal changes of any merit would have taken place within Catholicism, the existence of godly, internal critics such as Erasmus notwithstanding.

In theory the Catholics did not change at all. The Council of Trent, a town now in northern Italy, met between 1545 and 1563 and adopted the motto *semper idem*, Latin for "always the same."

But in fact many changes took place. Men such as Cardinal Gasparo Contarini (1483–1542) did all they could to try and bring about internal reforms, and Contarini also corresponded at length with Calvin, about whom we shall read more in the next chapter. For a brief moment it also appeared that a Lutheran/Catholic meeting in the German town of Regensburg in 1541 might bring about some kind of truce or accommodation, but the theological gulf had become far too wide to span.

This meant that the Catholic Church had to do something. Many of the changes were aesthetic, in the same way that the church in England greatly improved its music in the fifteenth century in order to combat the theological threat posed by the Lollard followers of Wycliffe. Pope Paul III (reigned 1534–1549) did all he could to stamp out as much of the corruption as possible, to take away that excuse for defecting to the Protestants.

But Paul III's major innovation was evangelistic. In 1540 he approved a new Catholic missionary order to win people back to the old faith by persuasion. This was the Society of Jesus, founded in 1540, and known ever since as the Jesuits.

The Jesuit Order, which still exists, has been described as the shock troops of the Catholic Church, a description that had some justification. In zeal they were the equivalent of the many missionaries Calvin sent out from Geneva to aid the conversion of France, and with the help of many Catholic princes, the Jesuits were highly effective. They were also dedicated missionaries overseas, as we shall see later.

Jesuits have always had bad press among Protestants, and with good reason since Catholic rulers used them to suppress Protestantism in many parts of Europe. Having said that, during this same period many Catholics were put to death in Protestant countries, especially in England, and in Cambridge, where I live, there is a large Catholic church entitled Our Lady and the English Martyrs, many of them being Jesuits put to death during the reign of Queen Elizabeth I. I think though when it comes to creating martyrs, all sides were equally guilty, and both Protestant and Catholic rulers killed Anabaptists.

While the Jesuits did not themselves engage in military warfare, one of the main reasons for their success was their highly martial sense of self-discipline, a ruthless regime of self-control that Jesuits have to exercise even today, though most Jesuits would now be on the theologically liberal end of the spectrum. The excesses of the fifteenth-century Borgia Popes horrified clean-living Catholics, and the founder of the Jesuits, the Spanish aristocrat Ignatius of Loyola (1491–1556), introduced iron discipline to his followers. His *Spiritual Exercises* are still read by Catholics, whether Jesuit or not, and his dictum "to serve and not to count the cost" is employed by Protestants as well as Catholics today.

In recent years some evangelicals have said that the Reformation was a shame. Of course, Catholics have been saying so since it happened. In one sense such Protestants have been misinterpreted, since what some mean is that it was a shame that the church ever disintegrated doctrinally to the extent that the Reformation was necessary. For others, alas, it is the first sign of ecumenical, confused thinking.

As an evangelical I would naturally reject such thinking, since it is surely obvious that the return to biblical truth in the Reformation was a wonderful act of God. But one could argue that the Reformation did the Catholic Church a huge amount of good as well.

One can see this in looking at the sad saga of the inward-looking Orthodox churches. For them there was no Reformation, and while it is fair to say that much of the cause of that was the Ottoman Muslim rule of so much of Orthodoxy's original heartland, it is not the case with Russia, since the Tsars were able to overthrow the Islamic yoke centuries earlier.

The Reformation gave Catholicism local competition, especially when, politically, it became evident that Protestantism could not be exterminated by brute force in Germany, let alone in other parts of central and western Europe that also converted to Protestantism. Catholicism was thus obliged to adapt to a rival in a manner that was not true of the Orthodox churches to the East. This inevitably helped renew Catholicism from within and, I would argue, benefited the Catholic Church as a result. So the Reformation, by forcing Catholicism to adapt, thus benefited everyone.

FIVE

The Reformation—
Succeeding Reformers

We will first look further at the background of the Reformation, consider other Reformers worthy of our attention, then close with some relevant conclusions.

The Politics of the Reformation

In this book and in another one I have written (*Five Leading Reformers*) I have agreed with those secular writers who have given much weight to the political background of the Reformation. Even though they are approaching the subject from an altogether different angle from that of my evangelical perspective, I do think they are right to say that politics played a huge role in the events of that era. Where I differ is that I would see God using the politics of sixteenth-century central Europe in the same way in which He employed both godly kings like Josiah and nonbelievers such as Cyrus to accomplish His purposes.

In the West today, especially in the USA where there is separation between church and state, we forget that until comparatively recently the two were inexorably linked. This is especially true of *Christendom*, the Catholic western and central part of Europe, where state and church were enmeshed in a way that we would find extraordinary now.

As we shall see in this chapter and later on in the book, even the Reformers found it difficult to disentangle the two. But as historians such as Lammin Sanneh at Yale and others have shown, the Reformation made inevitable not only the demise of Christendom but also the freedom of religion that we all now take for granted in the West.

Christendom was both a spiritual unit—the Catholic countries of Europe—but in a sense a political one as well. In the sixteenth century the Holy Roman Emperor, Charles V, was also, by a series of dynastic accidents, King Carlos of Spain and thus also ruler of most of South America, but also, again through dynastic chance, much of Italy as well. He had also inherited the Netherlands—today's Belgium as well as the present Netherlands—and what we now call Austria and the Czech Republic, then called Bohemia. He was therefore a very considerable figure and in addition was a man who took his Catholic faith very seriously.

Although both France and England were outside his vast domains, the French king had the title *Catholic King* from the Pope (the King of Spain was the *Most Catholic King*), and King Henry VIII of England had the papal title of *Defender of the Faith*. All of western and central Europe, therefore, was officially Catholic, and the various kings and princes rigidly enforced Catholic orthodoxy within their domains, with heretics savagely persecuted.

In other words, the spiritual and the political went together. If you lived in Saxony, for example—the region from which Luther came—you were automatically, from birth, both a subject of the Holy Roman Emperor and a member of the Catholic Church.

What follows might seem a little complex, but in God's providence it all proved more than helpful to the survival of the Reformation. So be patient, and get a good historical atlas to see what a patchwork quilt Europe looked like around 1500.

Germany, I should explain, did not exist as such until 1870. But apart from areas such as Bohemia, where most people were Czechs, or the Netherlands, where people were what we now call Dutch or Belgian, the bulk of the Holy Roman Empire was ethnically German, until its final fall in 1806.

However, under the emperor were literally hundreds of smaller mini-states, owing him allegiance. The seven most important of these were called *electorates*, since their ruler was one of the seven people who elected a new emperor on the death of his predecessor. One of these was the ruler of Saxony, in the eastern part of the Empire, and he had the title *Elector of Saxony*. Another was the Elector Palatine, in the Rhineland, in whose dominions the ancestors of millions of present-day Americans once lived.

There were also various dukedoms, such as Hesse, and in many parts of the Empire, towns were directly under the emperor, and these were called *Imperial Free Cities*. Next, Catholic bishops in much of the Empire were also secular rulers, three of the most eminent also being Electors, with the most important being the Archbishop and Elector of Mainz. Finally, some knights also owed direct allegiance to the emperor, with their domains often being no more than a castle and a few acres.

So what does all this have to do with the Reformation?

The answer is, a very great deal.

Then as now Catholics across the world owed spiritual allegiance to the Pope. But as Empire and Pope were linked, and as the Popes would not hesitate to exercise their rights in all of Europe, many of the local rulers were becoming increasingly disgruntled with what they felt was outside interference in their own domains. This was the case in much of the Holy Roman Empire, where local rulers were beginning to want to gain power at the emperor's expense as well.

So by 1517 there were many Electors and minor princes and knights in the Empire who hated both the Pope and emperor. Thus when Luther came along and said all this was unnecessary, he was speaking to a more than receptive audience. Luther meant his message spiritually, of course, but politically it had major ramifications, in that it meant that many a German ruler or free city need owe no allegiance to a foreign Pope and to his main political defender, the emperor.

In England and in the Scandinavian countries, the kings wanted total control over their own kingdoms. Interfering with this was papal interference on who got what major abbey or bishopric. Linked with that was the power of the land since rich abbots were also major land-owners who might insist on giving the profits not to the king in taxes but to the Pope, hundreds of miles away in Rome.

In addition, as we have seen, the Pope was also a major ruler in central Italy—the Patrimony of St. Peter or Papal States, a mini-kingdom that lasted until the unification of Italy in the nineteenth century. This made matters complex because while Luther was nailing his theses to the door in Wittenberg, the Italian peninsula was at war. The Holy Roman Emperor ruled over Milan and the King of Spain over the Kingdom of Naples. Uniquely, during this period the ruler of Milan and Naples was, during the Reformation, the same person, the Emperor Charles V. Not only that, but the French kings also thought they had a hereditary claim to all these places. This meant that the Pope, as secular ruler of the Papal States, was during this conflict piggy in the middle. The wars saw French and imperial troops charging all over his territories on the way to somewhere else.

Thus when King Henry VIII wanted to divorce his wife, Catherine of Aragon, who was also Charles V's aunt, it was a profoundly political issue as well as a spiritual one. The Pope was suffering from imperial forces rampaging in his territories and on one occasion even sacking Rome itself. Such actions were for political reasons, for no one was a more devout Catholic in the spiritual sense than Emperor Charles V. Henry's asking for a divorce from Charles's aunt meant military and political suicide for the Pope, so he naturally refused. This enraged Henry VIII, who was desperate for a divorce, and so when a young theologian named Thomas Cranmer told him that to go to the Pope was quite unnecessary, Henry leaped at the chance. Once again political dilemmas created profoundly spiritual opportunities.

By Faith and by Scripture Alone

People ask why there are so many Protestant denominations. I think that these two pivots of Reformation thought, both returns to Christianity's origins, say it all.

Becoming a Christian is a matter of conviction, not of ancestry or geography. Therefore an act of our will is involved, a conscious act. Becoming a Christian is not just something that happens to us, like being born or having blue eyes or brown hair.

Second, Scripture is our guide, not what an external source—the Vatican or the tradition of the ages, for example—tells us to believe. This ties in with another great Reformation rediscovery—the priesthood of all believers. Only Christ is our Mediator with God, not a human institution; and there is no priestly caste since Christ is our only and all-sufficient High Priest.

So it is natural that divisions occur on what Luther correctly described as *indifferent matters*—the form of church government, whether or not we baptize children or believers only, and a myriad host of other issues on that level.

Denominations are by their very nature man-made, groups of believers who choose a particular kind of belief or emphasis. This is why there are so many Protestant denominations and one Roman Catholic Church. We Protestants do not believe in the Pope as God's authority on earth but rather believe that the Word of God, the Bible, speaks to us directly, not through human intermediaries. But we do not always agree on how to interpret particular issues. For example, some Christians believe in baptism for believers only, others in covenant baptism for the children of believers. So denominations arose because of our interpretations of Scripture and because we reject the

Catholic belief in an infallible Pope who keeps Catholics in one single denomination or church.

Does this matter? Ultimately I think not. All true evangelicals are united around the central truths of the Atonement and of the need for righteous living. When the divisions began after 1517—notably between Luther and Zwingli, the Swiss Reformer, on the issue of the nature of Communion, the Lord's Supper—some were understandably perturbed by the failure to agree. But in the end the fact that they *did* agree on the most important of all matters—the nature of salvation—put the debates on all secondary issues into perspective.

Where the issue of division did become tragic was with the advent of what historians call the Radical Reformation and the rise of the Anabaptists.

We have seen how political the Reformation had become. Princes protected those under their authority, and the Elector of Saxony helped prevent Luther from meeting the fate of Jan Hus.

However, the other side of the coin was that in Protestant areas the prince (king, duke) had a major say in the affairs of the church within his domain. No separation of church and state took place.

To a growing number of Christians this was simply wrong. Among them was Menno Simons (1496–1561), a leader who believed, like the Donatists centuries before, that the church consisted of true believers only, and not of those citizens living in a particular geographical area. Not only that, but Simons felt, as do all Baptists today, as well as evangelicals of many other persuasions, that baptism should be for believers only and not something that happens at birth, the latter being based not upon faith but upon geography, on where your parents are born.

When he was therefore baptized again—as a believer—this was, in the eyes of the official Protestant churches as well as the Catholic Church, tantamount to a second baptism since they regarded his first one as the only one that was valid. He had been *rebaptized*, hence the name *Anabaptist* (*ana* meaning "again"). This put him and all his followers out of bounds both doctrinally over the issue of baptism but also politically since they denied that the state was legitimately able to play a major role in the internal affairs of the church.

Consequently, from 1527 onward Anabaptists were put to death—usually by the gruesome death of being burned at the stake but sometimes by being drowned—by Protestant rulers as well as Catholic.

Nowadays Baptists are so strong globally—the Southern Baptist Convention is the biggest Protestant denomination in the USA, for example—that we forget the tiny, minority, and persecuted status with which they began.

John Calvin

It is hard for someone of Reformed belief to write objectively about John Calvin, for to many of us he is the towering genius of the Reformation, being not only its great theologian but, for example, through his sponsorship of the missions to France, one of its most powerful evangelists as well. As J. I. Packer, a major Reformed theologian of more recent times, has written, John Calvin (1509–1564) "orchestrated Protestant theology," although as Packer also concedes, Luther "wrote most of the tunes."

Calvin is, alas, today also one of the most disliked of the Magisterial Reformers. His role in the condemnation to death of the Unitarian Michael Servetus is always hurled against him, even though, as Alister McGrath reminds us, Calvin's role was only that of a legal consultant, and that, as I would remind my readers, was nothing compared to the encouragement Luther gave to German aristocrats to slaughter their rebellious peasants or to that of the Swiss Reformer Zwingli, who actually died while fighting on the battlefield.

Yet Calvin's influence is wider today than that of any of the other Reformers. Not only do Presbyterians follow in his footsteps, but so do millions of Protestant evangelicals in other denominations, even if they would not always describe themselves as being primarily Reformed theologically. Many a Baptist, Independent, Anglican, and

charismatic would hold large swaths of Calvin's theology and openly
admit their enormous debt to the way in which he helped them sys-
tematize biblical truth.

This is because Calvin did not just found denominations but also
a whole way of thinking about what the Bible teaches, and an entire
worldview that goes with that. Back in the 1990s I knew a large number
of Pentecostals, for instance, who while rejecting Calvin's interpretation
of God's grace would say that their worldview as Christians living in a
secular society was nonetheless entirely Calvinist in scope.

Calvin was originally French, training as a lawyer. In 1533 he was
converted, and since Protestantism was still highly suspect in Paris,
Calvin had to flee to what is now French-speaking Switzerland, that
region being a mix of city-states or cantons not long independent
from the power of the Catholic Dukes of Savoy and allied to the Swiss
Confederation but not fully part of it.

It was not until eight years and many vicissitudes later—including
a spell in Strasbourg—that Calvin ended up permanently in Geneva,
the city-state with which he is most associated.

Calvin, as he was of the Magisterial Reformation persuasion,
wanted to create a godly city filled with Christian citizens devoted to
proper faith and practice. In this he was typical of his time, seeing the
state—in this case the Geneva City Council—as the instrument to
ensure godliness among the population. The key thing to remember
is that everyone else—Protestant and Catholic alike—took that view
at that time, and it was not until the late seventeenth century, after
150 years of religious war and carnage, that people even considered a
different point of view.

Calvin's real contribution to faith therefore was not so much Geneva
itself as what he wrote and thought while living there—he was not
granted full citizenship for many years after he arrived.

He made Christian doctrine easier to understand. This is called
systematic theology, and no one did it better than Calvin. His most
famous work, which he updated regularly, is his multi-volume *Insti-*

tutes, which is still read widely today. He also wrote commentaries on individual books of the Bible, which are also still studied.

Calvin is often misinterpreted as writing mainly about predestination, the biblical doctrine that explains the mechanism of salvation. While he did indeed write about it, so did Luther, who came to exactly the same theological conclusions. Yet we associate the doctrine with Calvin, not Luther, and also forget that, for example, it is historically a teaching also strongly associated with Augustine, and therefore, historically speaking, not really one that one can properly describe as "Calvinist" at all since it was already ancient when he expounded it. Not only that, but, as all of us in the Reformed part of evangelical Christianity would argue, Calvin simply found it plainly in Scripture. Calvin would argue—as would all who agree with him—that he was merely doing what Paul was expounding in epistles such as Romans and Ephesians. All of us are rebels and sinners against God, and it is a sign of the love and mercy of God that He chooses any of us to become Christians at all. In that sense, as the late Bethan Lloyd-Jones would put it, his position on this is not so much "Reformed" as simply "biblical." (Because of this, John MacArthur once told me, "I like your grandmother!")

As Alister McGrath reminds us, Calvin put predestination not into the theology of conversion but into his exposition of the person of God. This is, of course, where it belongs. But it is a doctrine that is hard for some to accept since we have a natural tendency to look at things from a human point of view rather than from that of God Himself, which is what the Bible does.

Some of Calvin's most enthusiastic followers were in Britain, where he influenced countless Puritans over the course of centuries. Had English history gone differently—had King Edward VI lived longer, for example, or even outlived his persecuting Catholic sister Mary—the Church of England would itself have become Puritan since that is the direction in which its leaders, such as Thomas Cranmer, were taking it before Edward's premature death. As it is, we know that the Puritans continued as a minority, and when they actually ruled Britain in 1649–1660, their continued minority status meant that they were unable to effect permanent change.

As a result, we have the Puritan half of the founding of what is now the USA—I put it like that for reasons we will see later in looking at early American history. One can therefore say that without understanding Calvin you cannot understand America since it was his thinking—on issues such as the Protestant work ethic, just to take one example—that so influenced the Puritans and thus shaped today's USA.

Zwingli and the Swiss Reformation

One of the Protestant leaders who did not hesitate to execute Anabaptists was Ulrich (Huldreich) Zwingli (1484–1531), the great Swiss Reformer. He was one of the early Reformers to be both a firm Protestant and at the same time break with Luther, the founding father of the Reformation, over key doctrinal issues. Zwingli also poses a problem for us since he literally died in battle, a soldier as well as a preacher, doing what he thought was best to defend the Reformation against its enemies.

His area of difference with Luther was over Communion, the Lord's Supper. The Catholic Church had taken an almost magical view, regarding Christ as *literally* present in the elements each time Communion (Mass) was celebrated—and naturally only a priest could act as the celebrant or presiding officer at the Table. Luther believed in a kind of halfway house view: Christ was really but not corporally present.

To Zwingli, as to countless evangelicals since, this was still too superstitious. He felt that Communion was a commemoration of Christ's death until His return and that the service was, while a wonderfully powerful and spiritual act, symbolic and not literal. Calvin believed the same as Zwingli.

The Reformation in Britain

Humanly speaking, the Reformation in Britain owed everything to two immoral rulers. The first of these was King Henry VIII. He had a daughter, Mary, but his Queen Catherine of Aragon (part of Spain) had delivered him no sons. Today we know, ironically, that it is the man who determines the gender of the child, but that is a recent discovery, and for most of history the baby's sex was seen firmly as the fault (or otherwise) of the mother. He therefore wished to divorce Catherine and marry a young lady of the court, Anne Boleyn, whose sister Mary had been his mistress.

Henry had originally been given permission to marry Catherine by special papal dispensation. The reason was that she was the widow of his deceased brother Arthur, and the marriage, as with all royal weddings in those days, had been made for matters of state and diplomacy.

Henry now wanted the current Pope to dispense with his predecessor's earlier dispensation and to declare the marriage void. But here there were grave political complications. Henry's wife Catherine of Aragon (a Spanish princess) was the aunt of the Holy Roman Emperor Charles V, Luther's main political opponent in Germany. The Pope, in addition to being the spiritual head of the Roman Catholic Church, also ruled over most of central Italy (and continued to do so until the mid-nineteenth century). While Charles V was a devout Catholic, he opposed the *political* policy of the Pope as an Italian ruler, and on one occasion Charles's troops actually sacked Rome and forced the Pope to flee for safety. As a result, no Pope was going to oppose Charles V, the most powerful secular ruler in Europe. As a result of that, Henry VIII's cause was sunk—the Pope would never agree to give a divorce to the husband of the Holy Roman Emperor's aunt and thereby risk Charles's wrath.

So despite the best efforts of Henry's chief minister, Cardinal Thomas Wolsey—who, just to make life interesting, was also the Pope's Legate to England—to obtain the divorce the king wanted, the royal claim was always going to be rejected, and on political grounds, not spiritual.

It looked as if there would be a permanent impasse. But then some early Protestants suggested to the king that although the Pope, who had given Henry the title *Defender of the Faith* for opposing Luther, was head of the Catholic Church, nonetheless the Pope should not have the right to say whom the king could and could not marry. One of these was a promising young Cambridge academic named Thomas Cranmer (1489–1556). This was exactly what Henry wanted to hear. So he split from Rome, declared the Church in England independent (it has been the official Church *of* England ever since), divorced Catherine, married Anne Boleyn, and theoretically at least took Britain into the Reformation. Cranmer was duly rewarded, becoming the first Protestant Archbishop of Canterbury.

Cranmer was a genuine Protestant, and so too were many in his circle. But Henry's motivation had been political, not spiritual. Anne gave him a daughter—later to be justly famous as England's great Queen Elizabeth I. But Henry was only interested in a son to perpetuate the still shaky Tudor dynasty. In little time Anne was divorced and beheaded, and Henry married Jane Seymour, who died in childbirth, giving Henry a son, Edward. So while England was nominally Protestant, doctrinally Henry hardly changed at all. Cranmer had to walk a permanent tightrope, and Protestantism in terms of serious doctrinal change was not really introduced until Edward acceded to the throne as a boy—King Edward VI—in 1547.

Edward was a genuine Protestant, and for six years England was working toward being a truly Protestant country, with a Church of England that was not unlike its Calvinist neighbor to the north, the Church of Scotland. This is when the real Reformation began in England, when those who had true faith were able to do something about it for the first time.

But then Edward died young in 1553, only sixteen years old. An attempt to impose his godly cousin Jane Grey as his successor failed after just nine days, and Henry's daughter by Catherine of Aragon, the zealously Catholic Mary I, became queen. She put Protestants to death—having many burned at the stake—and had a nominal marriage to her cousin, King Philip of Spain.

Thankfully for Protestantism, Mary died childless in 1558, and her half-sister, Henry's daughter by Anne Boleyn, Elizabeth I, became queen, this time with a long reign, until 1603.

Elizabeth was a Protestant. But I think it fair to say that in her case her Protestantism was a tribal badge of identity and loyalty to her mother. She persecuted Catholics, but she also strongly opposed the Puritans, regarding them as extremists. She supported the middle of the road in the Church of England, and the extraordinary doctrinal mix that denomination is today is very much a result of the Elizabethan compromise. England was safe from Catholic despotism, and Elizabeth was careful to work with Parliament, in which many Puritans sat. But the doctrinal enthusiasm of King Edward VI's reign was not restored.

In other words, the Reformation in England was a political event, imposed initially for entirely state reasons by a small elite at the top. As leading British historian Eamon Duffy—the supervisor of Crossway author Mark Dever's definitive work on Richard Sibbes—has pointed out, it was well into Elizabeth's reign that we could honestly say that England at grass roots was a Protestant country, as Catholicism lingered on for decades at popular level, for much longer than many Protestant writers realized in the past. (Duffy is the Catholic author of the award-winning *The Stripping of the Altars*, a discussion of how England slowly did become Protestant.)

In Scotland the Reformation was much more of a grass-roots affair, helped by the disgust of the Protestant nobility at the foreign rule of the mother of Mary, Queen of Scots. King James V had died young, leaving an infant daughter, Mary, who nominally succeeded him on the throne. But she spent her childhood in France, being married briefly to one of the last Valois kings of that country. The true ruler was her mother, the Frenchwoman Mary of Guise, who was widely disliked. Eventually Mary returned home but soon found herself in trouble, not least because of her unsuitable choice of successive husbands. In the end she was deposed in favor of her infant son, King James VI, who was raised as a Protestant (and who in 1603 became King James I of England).

As a result, John Knox (d. 1572—his exact birth year is unknown), the giant of the Protestant Reformation in Scotland, was able to introduce a far more doctrinal, Reformed Protestantism into Scotland. Not only that, but while the Church of Scotland is the established church there, the state has no say in who its leaders are, nor in its doctrines, unlike England, where all senior appointments are still made by the state and where major doctrinal changes still need Parliamentary approval.

Why All These Denominations?

We have seen how Luther returned us to *sola scriptura* and to *sola fidei*. No longer was a priestly caste needed to mediate between believers and God, and ordinary Christians could now read the Word of God in their own language, without the need of a priest to interpret it for them.

It did not take very long for the Reformers to come to different positions on a whole wide range of issues, however. Now that there was no longer one monolithic church to enforce a sole interpretation, Christians increasingly used their biblical freedom to come up with slightly divergent views on matters such as church government, baptism, and Holy Communion.

This remains very much the case today, as we see from the bewildering array of denominations around the world. When as a Briton I visit the USA to teach every year, I am always coming across denominations of whose existence I had never before heard, since groups exist in the USA that are to be found nowhere else.

The same is true all over Africa, for example, and even in Scotland. How many outside that latter country know the exact doctrinal stances of the Associated Free Presbyterian Church of Scotland? Can you tell why it is not part of the still existing Free Presbyterian Church of Scotland? Do you know why, in turn, that denomination split from the very much remaining Free Church of Scotland?

In Britain we have many Calvinistic (or Grace) Baptists who are their own denomination. In the USA many Southern Baptists are now also becoming equally Reformed in their theology—thanks in part to such rising stars as Mark Dever and Al Mohler. But not so long ago such things were thought by many to be a contradiction in terms! So too were Calvinistic Methodists, not, I think, a group at all well known in the USA but who have existed for centuries in Wales.

Does all this matter? I think not. It is surely a natural outgrowth of the freedoms rediscovered at the Reformation, one that led to Lutherans, Calvinists, Anglicans, and many other such groups very early on in Protestantism. Nor do we need artificial ecumenism—pretending we do not really have differences after all—to keep us together. If we are evangelical—faithful to the gospel—we know instinctively that what unites us in Christ is far more important than the lesser distinctive doctrines that separate us. Luther himself realized this when he spoke of inessential matters, doctrines such as church government that, while they can get us highly exercised, do not actually make a difference on whether or not someone goes to heaven. Baptists may joke that other people baptize their own way whereas they baptize God's way, but evangelical Baptists know they will see equally evangelical Presbyterians in heaven.

Why Do We Follow Whom We Follow?

There is a sense in which this is a silly question, for as the old chorus goes, "for the Bible tells me so."

In fact, though, since the Protestants broke up into different denominational groups almost as soon as the Reformation began, this became a more difficult thing to argue regarding issues such as church government or baptism, upon which equally sincere and genuine believers radically disagreed.

But a more worrying trend emerged, one that I think is still a danger to even those of us who profess to be evangelicals, who believe ourselves fully to be gospel-based, Christ-centered Christians. We may also in effect resurrect the Catholic doctrine of saints as special people and the authority of the church to be equal to that of Scripture. How so?

How often are we convinced of something because a preacher is winsome rather than because he is truly biblical? We believe, as we certainly should, in an infallible and inerrant Bible. But do we in effect often make our favorite preachers infallible too? And even if, as we would hope, they are correct, do we still look at the passage upon which they have preached ourselves, to use the apostle Paul's challenge to "test everything" so we can be sure (1 Thessalonians 5:21)?

We all have heroes, and it is very easy to follow the doctrinal views of those whom, in many ways entirely rightly, we revere. It was my maternal grandfather Dr. D. Martyn Lloyd-Jones's nightmare that someone would agree with something simply because he, Dr. Lloyd-Jones, had said it. He would do all possible at mealtimes to stir up his doting grandchildren to disagree with him. He would often say outrageous things that he knew to be nonsense to make sure that we believed what we did on *biblical* grounds, not because he was our much loved grandfather. There are plenty of great Christian leaders whom I—along with millions of others—revere deeply. But when I listen to them, I always recall how appalled Dr. Lloyd-Jones would have been if I agreed with them without checking what they said against the Scriptures.

In fact, when he was a minister at a poor inner-city mission church in South Wales during the Depression, Martyn Lloyd-Jones would often find that there was no correlation between education and spiritual insight. In his Bible class for men, the poverty-stricken dockyard worker was as likely to understand what Scripture was saying as the highly educated professional man.

It is right that Luther, Calvin, Cranmer, Knox, Zwingli, and others are our heroes. They were faithful pioneers for the truth, and many Reformers lost their lives for it. But they were not infallible, and looking down from heaven as now they do, they would not want us to make them into the Protestant equivalent of a Pope, six feet above all human contradiction. The same, of course, applies to later heroes such as George Whitefield, Jonathan Edwards, C. H. Spurgeon, Martyn Lloyd-Jones, and his great contemporaries Francis Schaeffer and Billy Graham.

It all comes back to two things. First, as humans we must recognize our weakness in granting *too* great a status to those who are deservedly our heroes since we are all fallible by definition. Second, it is *Scripture alone/sola scriptura* that determines all our doctrine, all our beliefs, what we follow and why. The Reformation rediscovered that great truth, but even there we believe it not because the Reformers did before us but because that is what the Bible teaches about itself.

Why Do We Believe What We Do?

As evangelicals, this ought to be, according to that wonderful American expression I have come to love, a no-brainer. We are Bible-believing Christians.

This is vital because we as evangelicals can all too easily lull ourselves into thinking that as Scripture-based Christians we would never make the same mistakes as, say, Roman Catholics or members of cultic groups or base what we believe on accumulated ecclesiastical tradition or on the interpretations of a leading man. Yet while we correctly reject such notions in theory, sadly in practice we follow the same path all the time. Our denominational traditions can be as important to us as the teachings of the Mother Church are to Roman Catholics. Because we do not say this officially, we can all too easily forget the trap and jump straight into it.

Even so-called Calvinists like me need to be wary of this! A story will show this—not important in and of itself but symbolic of how the past is used and misused in ways that we as evangelical Christians do not realize we are doing.

Some decades back an American preacher then in Britain, Dr. R. T. Kendall, proposed in a book that Calvin only actually believed four of the five "points of Calvinism" and that one of the points had in fact been invented subsequently by later English Puritans.

The uproar was immense! Articles were composed, books written, conferences convened. But to an outside observer like me, two debates were in fact taking place, not just one.

The first—what did Calvin *actually* believe—was a fair one and worthy of the scholarly debate that had ensued. Like Crossway author Mark Dever I tend to believe Calvin *did* believe in all five of his "points," but that is a side issue.

But the second debate was a strange one. What the British, American, and Australian Calvinists who spoke against Kendall were in effect saying was, "Calvin *must* have believed all five, because all five are true, and because they are true, Calvin, who was never wrong, must have believed in them himself."

This was surely a sad and rather circular argument for evangelical Protestants! While Calvin probably did argue for all five of them, what matters is *what the Bible teaches*, as I tried in my own small way—I was only a student at the time—to argue as my contribution to the debate. Not only that, but as I wrote in a letter, if all five points are scriptural, then they are true, and if Calvin only believed in four of them, *then Calvin was wrong*. Needless to say, the last part of that did not go down well with some.

Simultaneously, Calvinist Baptists in Britain were having an argument in print with Calvinist charismatics (some of whom were also Calvinist Baptist charismatics!) on whether you can call yourself Reformed and believe in the continuation of the miraculous sign gifts such as tongues and prophecy. The British Calvinist (or Grace) Baptists were saying that this was impossible since Calvin was a firm cessationist, and that being the case, being both Calvinist and charismatic at the same time was impossible.

All this was part of a larger row on whether or not Martyn Lloyd-Jones, in rejecting the cessationist position in his book *Joy Unspeakable*, was himself biblical, which we shall examine later.

In their understanding of Calvin, the Calvinist Baptists were, of course, entirely correct. But as Presbyterians would properly remind us, he also rejected the entire Baptist position as well. So on *that* understanding, being a Calvinist Baptist is also a historical impossibility since Calvin was a paedobaptist through and through.

It was Mark Dever, then a student and now one of the leading Baptists with a thoroughgoing Reformed theology, who struck me at the time as one of the few who saw things with crystal clarity. As he pointed out then and preaches now, what matters is what the clear teaching of Scripture is upon the matter. If what Calvinist Baptists believe in is the *biblical* theology of baptism and the *scriptural* teaching on grace and salvation, then they are right on *both* issues, even if Calvin would agree with them on one issue and not on the other. Although Dever disagrees with Lloyd-Jones on the issue of spiritual gifts, the principle remains the same. It is *what Scripture says that counts*, even if that means realizing that our heroes of the past, whether Calvin or Lloyd-Jones, are fallible, just like the rest of us. Only Scripture is inerrant—we are not.

Who Still Rules the Church?

Earlier we saw that the Donatists asked the question, "Who rules the church?" During the Reformation that issue was never fully resolved. As the leading American church historian Timothy George reminds us, men such as Calvin, Luther, Zwingli, and Cranmer were all part of what is described as the *Magisterial* Reformation, whereas Anabaptists such as Menno Simons were not. All this is a debate that went back to the fateful decision in 325 at Nicea to allow the Emperor Constantine to have a role in the internal affairs of the Christian church.

As we will see, in a place such as the USA this is now an issue that has been decided, and in countries such as Britain the two sides agreed to differ with legal rights extended to both sides.

But during the Reformation what one could call the Constantinian position very much held sway, much to the detriment of that brave minority who embraced what I would describe as an updated version of the Donatist view.

We saw earlier that politics played a pivotal part in the Reformation's taking place at all. Looking at it from an evangelical perspective, I would say that what God did was to take the selfish desires of sinful rulers—Henry VIII's wanting to get divorced for lustful and dynastic reasons, for example—and used them to bring about His own purposes, in the same way that He used secular rulers such as Pharaoh or varied Assyrian kings to do His will in biblical times.

Be that as it may, the result was a continued interdependence of church and state that made any kind of formal separation unthinkable. The Constantinian method prevailed, and, I think, with spiritually unhelpful consequences.

In much of Germany, for instance, some Catholic clergy were secular rulers as well as grand ecclesiastical prelates. The Archbishop of Salzburg, for example, for whom Mozart wrote music, was also the lay ruler of a large principality until as late as 1803. The Archbishops of Mainz—one of whom Luther opposed—were not just secular princes but also among the seven Electors who chose the Holy Roman Emperor.

In other parts of Europe the situation was different in that the ruler was a layman. But even there, from the 1550s through to the 1640s, how you worshiped God was entirely up to the whim of the local prince. The principle was *cuius region, eius religio*—"whose territory, his religion." If your prince was a Protestant, so was the principality in which you lived, and likewise if he was a Catholic.

In England this could be dangerous for those who had a sure faith either one way or the other. King Henry VIII was nominally Protestant but Catholic in practice. His son King Edward VI was a godly and devout Protestant. His elder daughter Queen Mary I was a persecuting Catholic, and his younger daughter Queen Elizabeth I was a firm Protestant.

In France there were decades of civil war in which thousands died. The decadent Catholic kings oscillated between accommodating the growing Protestant (or Huguenot) community and persecuting them. The heir of the last Valois king was a Protestant, Henry of Navarre. He eventually became king as Henry IV but made a political conversion to Catholicism to ensure his throne. This always makes me wonder what in fact he actually believed. He granted toleration to the Huguenots by the Edict of Nantes in 1598, but what one king could give, another could remove, and this happened when his descendant King Louis XIV revoked the Edict in the 1680s and caused thousands of Protestant Frenchmen to have to flee, many to British-ruled North America.

In much of Europe, your national identity came to be your religious identity. So Poland became a devoutly Catholic country, which it is to this day, and Britain became equally strongly Protestant, especially since Britain's enemies were Catholic nations such as Spain or France.

None of this is biblical since where you are born is irrelevant to Scripture and to the doctrines of conversion, which occurs through being born again through the work of the Holy Spirit, not because of geography or biological parentage. Many parts of Europe still have state churches, and in others churches paid for by state funds. But Western Europe, as opposed to the USA where church and state are firmly separate, is now one of the most secular places on earth.

SIX

The Age of Expansion and Revival

"G o into all the world and proclaim the gospel to the whole creation" (Mark 16:15).

This command of Jesus to go to every nation with the gospel of salvation is a verse we surely all know. I imagine too that most of us attend churches that at least pray regularly for missions and, I would hope, have a significant number of members serving God overseas in some capacity or another. I am on the Overseas Missions Group of my church, for example, and my mother is on the missions committee at the church she and my father attend. Maybe you fill a similar role at yours.

So it might surprise you to discover that Protestant churches took a long time to get going on overseas missions and that the first post-Reformation wave of missionary endeavor was that of the Catholic Church. But to our shame as evangelicals this is in fact the case. Once the Catholic Church found itself under pressure in Europe from the growth of Protestant Christianity, one of the first things it did was to engage in active overseas evangelism, bringing the gospel to peoples who had either never heard it before or to countries where it had not been preached for many centuries.

The Catholic Missions: Bringing the Gospel to Asia

As evangelicals we tend to have bad memories of the Jesuit Order, since in Europe Catholic rulers used the Jesuits ruthlessly to persecute and suppress Protestants. To be fair, in Anglican England it was the Jesuits who were put to death. However, when it comes to bringing the message of the Christian faith to Chinese, Indians, many tribes of Latin America, and other places, it was Jesuits, not Protestants, who were the pioneers. As we shall see, evangelicals eventually caught up, but that was some way off.

One of the great tragedies of the Christendom mentality at that time was that cross-cultural missions had long since been something of the past. Europeans did not neglect the active evangelism of earlier centuries, but they only evangelized other Europeans—the Baltic peoples, for example, who converted much later to Christianity than other parts of that continent. As for sending missionaries to Africa or Asia, that simply no longer happened.

Two things, I feel, had produced this change.

First of all, as the expression goes, trade follows the flag, and in many cases so too did the Christian message. This was the dawn of the era of Western colonial and economic expansion. Columbus rediscovered America not long before the Reformation (a coincidence?), and soon Europeans from Spain, Portugal, and England were beginning the European conquest and settlement of South and North America. India too was being settled, though the Portuguese colonies in India were small, and it was not until the eighteenth century that the major European conquest of South Asia began. Spain colonized the Philippines (named after King Philip of Spain), and Portugal gained footholds in China, such as Macau. Trade with Japan prospered briefly, and

what is called Japan's Open Century began, with Protestant Dutchmen
and Catholic Portuguese merchants vying both for trade and converts
in that country.

Especially interesting in many ways was what happened in China.
Here the powerful Qing (or Manchu) emperors restricted foreign trade
to southern ports, and apart from Macau no part of China fell under
European rule until the nineteenth century. Resourceful Jesuit mis-
sionaries, notably the scholar Matteo Ricci (1552–1610), reintroduced
China to Christianity.

The story of the Jesuit mission has often been told in terms of Ricci's
major scientific endeavors and of the way in which skilled Jesuits were
able to hold significant positions at the Imperial Court. Less known are
their attempts to make Christianity culturally relevant to the Chinese
and the dispute that they had as a result with the Dominican missionaries, who felt that the Jesuits had compromised too far in the
process. (The exact issue was the extent to which one could take part
in ceremonies to honor ancestors and the correct name by which God
should be called. The Dominicans felt that the word employed by the
Jesuits was too rife with pagan connotations.)

In turn this is usually shown as a picture of European crassness and
of papal interference. But I think it raises fascinating gospel and mis-
siological issues that remain relevant for us today in the twenty-first
century as evangelicals, both abroad and at home as well.

A Ghanaian Christian once told me that in his church they preferred
a piano and hymns to drums and contemporary songs. This seemed
odd to me, but his reason was interesting. Drums represented the old,
repressive paganism from which they had been rescued at the time of
their conversion. Pianos were certainly not Ghanaian, but they were
new, a change from the past, and therefore symbolized the new birth
they had experienced in Jesus. How could a white Westerner like me
dare to disagree? My friend's reaction may have been unusual, and I
know Christians from other countries, including within Africa, who
love putting Christian words to popular music, in the same way that
Luther used the tunes from drinking songs when writing his hymns.

But the point is an interesting one, nonetheless. Christianity is different from local tribal faiths, and it is important not to confuse the two, as syncretistic versions of the faith are prone to do.

In a 2006 issue of *The Tie*, the Southern Baptist Theological Seminary magazine, a contributor noticed that when he tried to be cool, the inner-city kids just laughed at him. When he just preached the gospel, they listened.

This is a biblical issue, one with which the early church wrestled, as we see both from the book of Acts and from the epistles. What role did circumcision play, for instance? What *in practice* did it mean to be a Greek to the Greeks and a Jew to the Jews? What if some Greek customs were borderline? I know we talk about meat offered to idols in other contexts, but does that debate here apply as well?

How far should we go in terms of adapting language to suit the people we are evangelizing? What compromises the gospel, and what simply puts it in words that our audience can comprehend? What is being helpful, and what is a step too far? This is a fascinating issue, and one that has not gone away, from the dawn of Christianity through to the first cross-cultural missions outside Europe to our own postmodern confused days.

One of the other major Jesuit missionaries was Francis Xavier (1506–1552). His primary mission field was also in Asia, in India (where the church today is flourishing, albeit under severe Hindu persecution) and in Japan (where it is as tiny as ever). In fact, Japan has been nicknamed the exception to the famous dictum that the blood of the martyrs is the seed of the church.

When Xavier began his mission to Japan, there were so many converts, it looked as if Japan was on the way to becoming a Christian country. But, alas, it was a false dawn. The ability to spread Christianity was a result of the benign political environment there, but this was to prove very temporary. Once the powerful Tokugawa family was able to consolidate their power in the country after a long period of internal strife, they established themselves permanently as shoguns, a position analogous to being a hereditary prime minister, with the emperor being a mere cipher.

The Tokugawa opposed Western infiltration of any kind—whether Catholic Portuguese or Protestant Dutch, and Christianity and the West were, alas, seen as interlinked. As a result, the shoguns forbade Christianity and expelled the Westerners—except for one small treaty port—until Commodore Matthew Perry from the USA reopened Japan to the West in the 1850s, and the shoguns were overthrown.

A tiny nominal church remained, not even a shadow of the large Japanese church that had existed after the Jesuit missions. Today Japan is one of the most advanced and powerful countries in the world, but the Christian churches there remain pitifully small, far tinier and weaker than the enormous and rapidly expanding churches nearby in both China and South Korea. Japan in the twenty-first century is as resistant to Christianity as ever.

However, when we look at Korea—long a Japanese colony—we see something interesting. Since the Japanese were the hated imperial power, when Western Christian missionaries came there in the twentieth century—often American Presbyterians the Korean people, unlike so many others in Asia, did not associate Christianity with Western colonialism, since in this case the West was the innocent party. Now South Korea is one of the most Christian countries in Asia, with a powerful and vibrant Protestant community that is sending thousands of its own people abroad in evangelism. Japan may have resisted the gospel, but Korea, its former colony, is embracing it.

The Heart Has Its Reasons

There was one other major development that we as evangelical Christians should not overlook. This was the phenomenon of Jansenism, a considerable renewal movement within the Catholic Church in France and the Netherlands in the seventeenth and eighteenth centuries.

This group was initially named for a bishop of Ypres, Cornelius Jansen. Although they were Catholics, they disliked the arid way in which Catholicism in the so-called Counter-Reformation had tried to combat Protestantism. They rediscovered the teachings of the great church father St. Augustine, who as we know took his own teaching in turn directly from the apostle Paul, as did the Protestant John Calvin during the Reformation. The Jansenists thus laid biblical stress on the sinful, fallen nature of the human race and upon the grace and love of God in bringing people to salvation through Jesus.

Needless to say, this was not well regarded by the Catholic hierarchy, whom the Jansenists were nominally trying to defend. Various papal decrees were hurled against them, and by the eighteenth century the power of the Jansenists was much diminished.

Although the Jansenists remained Catholic, it is clear that what they actually taught, believed in, and practiced was hardly different from the beliefs of Protestants.

The most famous Jansenist supporter was the mighty French thinker, scientist, and philosopher Blaise Pascal (1623–1662). Modern wristwatches and many modern hydraulic systems owe their ultimate origin to Pascal, and he is also the ancestor, through some of his calculating machines, of the computer.

To Pascal faith was personal, rather than the corporate kind that the Catholic Church effectively taught. He emphasized the need for the individual to be rescued by God from the depths of sin. His use of the word *fire* to describe his spiritual experiences has led some to call it a baptism of the Holy Spirit, and while one should be cautious about how to use such terminology, Pascal's writings on his inner spiritual experiences certainly interested twentieth-century evangelical writers such as Martyn Lloyd-Jones, who quoted from Pascal in his own sermons, shared in the book *Joy Unspeakable*.

Pascal is also interesting as a scientist who had strong Christian beliefs and who did not see being an intellectual as necessitating a rejection of the emotions. His famous saying, "the heart has its reasons that reason does not know" puts him in clear opposition to the deistic (and effectively atheistic) philosophers in France during the Enlightenment of the eighteenth century.

Here Pascal had much in common with the many evangelical thinkers and scientists who were at Oxford during and after his lifetime. We remember a scientist such as Isaac Newton, who was at Cambridge, but forget great practitioner scientists such as Robert Boyle at Oxford, one of the founders of British science and one of the large circle of Puritan Christians who eventually founded the Royal Society, still the premier scientific body outside of the USA today. Boyle was even more evangelical than Newton and was as interested in world mission as he was in science.

In fact, as Alister McGrath, Robert White, and Denis Alexander have all shown in their recent books, the origins of the *scientific* revolution in the West, called at the time in Britain the Great Instauration, were nearly all evangelical Christians, something that the humanist/atheistic world today seems to forget.

Protestants Catch Up:
Persecution and the Spread of Nonconformity

As we saw, the Protestant church took rather too long to catch up in terms of world mission and spreading the gospel cross-culturally.

Ironically, much of the missionary impetus originated in the persecution, tragically, of Protestants in states that were supposedly Protestant themselves, such as Britain. So we need to look at this first before we go on to see how Protestants did eventually catch up and begin the spread of biblical Christianity across the globe.

For a long time, it is said, many a poor Christian household would possess just two books: the Bible and *Pilgrim's Progress*. John Bunyan (1628–1688) came from Bedfordshire, a part of England with strong Puritan roots. He was a Congregationalist. This was a denomination that had been especially powerful during Britain's one period as a Republic, from 1649–1660 (known as the Commonwealth), under that great godly leader, Oliver Cromwell (1599–1658), the Lord Protector. As a consequence, Free Church or *nonconformist* Christians—those who did not conform to the Articles of the Church of England—were persecuted by King Charles II, who was restored to the throne in 1660 and who was a notoriously immoral king with strong Catholic sympathies.

Cromwell's head is in Sidney Sussex College, Cambridge in a secret location, so Royalists cannot find it and desecrate it. I am an alumnus of this college and often wondered if I was walking over his head! I also attended small group Bible studies on his old "staircase," where he lived as a student. He would be encouraged to know that strong evangelical/Reformed witness still exists in his old university.

Bunyan wrote much of *Pilgrim's Progress* while in jail. From 1662–1672 and again in 1676 he was in prison as a Protestant in a country that was itself officially Protestant.

His book still encourages us today—not just through Christian himself, but through supporting characters such as Mr. Valiant-for-Truth and horrors such as Doubting Castle and Giant Despair. It is a wonderfully encouraging and true picture of the Christian faith and thus typical of the realistic worldview of Puritan Christianity. Perhaps it is a telling sign of our times that one of the current top selling magazines today is *Vanity Fair*, the epitome of worldliness described in the novel.

In 1662 the king expelled all Puritans from the Church of England—the famous Richard Baxter of Kidderminster being one of them—and the persecution began.

This persecution did not limit itself to Britain. As my late father-in-law, John S. Moore, showed in over half a century of writing Virginia Baptist history, nonconformists were persecuted as much in the New World as in the Old, and Baptists and other dissenters were imprisoned for their beliefs.

This is because church and state were still, alas, seen as inextricably linked. We saw earlier that the Church of England was a political creation, and to the English ruling class, adherence to it remained a test of *political* loyalty. After the English Civil War of 1642–1649 and the subsequent Commonwealth period, being a nonconformist Christian was perceived as being the sign of a political radical, someone against the king and the restoration of the monarchy in 1660.

King Charles I had been a zealous believer in the "Divine Right of Kings" to rule despotically, and he had tried to rid himself of Parliament for as much of his reign as possible. His marriage—a rare, happy one for a British sovereign—to a devout French Catholic, Henrietta Maria, did not help. The main opposition to him was from godly Puritan politicians such as Cromwell and like-minded men, and when the latter took power in 1649 they tried—unsuccessfully as it turned out—to impose Christian personal morality on an immoral English people.

As a result, nonconformity in Britain was to be on the political left until well into the twentieth century—the British Labour Party was founded by an evangelical, a Methodist lay preacher named Keir Hardie—and on the side of liberty, democracy, and freedom. Several of the political groups in the Commonwealth period were avowedly socialist long before Marx, and in their case the politics of the Levellers, Diggers, and Fifth Monarchy Men actually derived from how they understood the Bible and interpreted the Scriptures.

All this was suppressed in 1660. Not until the nineteenth century would non-Anglicans have equal political rights.

King Charles II wisely did not convert to Catholicism until his deathbed. He had numerous illegitimate children—from some of whom Princess Diana was descended, and thus her son Prince William—but no legitimate heirs. He was thus succeeded by his brother James, Duke of York (for whom New York is named). James II had had an earlier Protestant wife, but he was himself a Catholic, and so was his current Italian wife. He tried to impose monarchical rule, as his father Charles I had done, and the Protestant (Anglican) establishment feared both despotism and "popery" or Catholic rule. James was thus forced to flee in 1688, and his Protestant daughter, Mary, by his first wife, was placed upon the throne in 1689 with her Dutch Calvinist husband, who now became King William III. He was also Prince of

Orange, a small French principality, and as a result Protestant loyalists in Northern Ireland are called Orangemen to this day, as Protestants were on the winning side in the Battle of the Boyne in Ireland in 1691, which prevented James's return. 1688 was called the Glorious Revolution, a successful military coup that prevented Britain from the far worse kinds of revolution that erupted in continental Europe, such as in France a century later.

Thankfully for the many nonconformists in Britain, the new post-1689 government realized that when it came to Catholic James versus Protestant William and Mary, the dissenting Protestant Christians were on their side. As a result, in 1689 Parliament passed an Act of Toleration, giving full freedom of worship to all Protestant Christians, but with full political rights still reserved for members of the Established Church. Catholics did not obtain full rights until the 1820s, but actual persecution of Catholics effectively now ceased. No longer would a Bunyan or a Smyth and Helwys be in danger of imprisonment.

Significantly for future history, France went in the opposite direction. King Louis XIV of France—the despotic "Sun King"—repealed the Edict of Nantes, by which Huguenot (Protestant) Christians in France enjoyed religious liberty. Now persecution resumed. Protestants fled to Britain, Protestant parts of Germany, and, increasingly, to the New World.

In any case many leading thinkers of the time finally realized that persecution was in all senses pointless, spiritually and politically.

The foremost writer along these lines was someone well-known in the USA for his political insights, the philosopher John Locke (1632–1704). Locke is famous today in America for his views on freedom, which much influenced the American Founding Fathers a few generations later. But his work also has profound Christian consequences.

In his *Epistle Concerning Toleration* Locke understood, for the first time in centuries, that if Christian conversion is an inward matter, then external pressure—persecution—is in fact pointless since someone can conform outwardly but be of the same original inner persuasion.

I have dealt with this at much more length in other books I have written and in a commissioned paper after 9/11 for the Strategy Unit of Tony Blair's Cabinet Office.

Locke was no evangelical despite his Calvinist roots. But as the late Roy Porter of London University wrote in his book on the Enlightenment, what is interesting about Locke and others of his time is that in Britain, the Enlightenment began *within* Protestantism, as opposed to outside and against it as in France. Admittedly, by the 1750s even British philosophers such as David Hume were coming out against the idea of miracles and were antagonistic to Christianity. But it is significant all the same that one of Locke's books was on the reasonableness of the Christian faith, even though we as evangelicals wish he would have made his arguments stronger. Freedom is a concept that benefits Christians, as it allows them to evangelize and worship freely, and this is something that was to be a theme running throughout Locke's work.

So while political freedom is a good thing, it led to religious freedom too, to the enormous benefit initially of Christians in the English-speaking world and then farther afield as well. No longer would you have to be a particular kind of Christian to be able to worship freely.

In due time, with the advent of the Enlightenment, freedom was expanded to the right not to believe in any kind of religion at all. But we should not forget in our post-Enlightenment times that religious and political freedom are historically intertwined and arrived together. Freedom is a *pre*-Enlightenment concept whatever the humanists and anti-religious might tell us today (and are deluded enough to forget themselves). It derives from the wish of thousands of seventeenth-century Christians to worship God as they felt His Word commanded and to obey God rather than men. Remove religious liberty, and you undermine the very construction upon which liberty is based.

How Christian Was Colonial America?

This concept did not come naturally, and, alas, even in the New World not all the Puritans realized it for themselves, even though they or their parents had been persecuted back in Britain or in whatever part of the Old World their families originated.

I think therefore that we can blame the Emperor Constantine rather than the Bible for the Salem witch trials! We should also not forget, as John S. Moore spent a lifetime showing, that godly dissenters were as persecuted in Virginia as they were back at home. Virginia was set up as an Anglican colony, and until independence that is what it remained. Also, many of the colonies were royal foundations and designed not for godliness but for worldly material prosperity. It is perhaps ironic that those states that began as refuges for godly people fleeing persecution are today far less Christian than those that began for secular purposes, but how far one can take that argument I am far from sure!

All too often we as evangelicals, living in tragically different times in the twenty-first century, when biblical Christianity seems under siege, look back at the early years of North America through rose-colored glasses. If, for example, Jerry Falwell were to return to Virginia in co-lonial times, he would as likely as not find himself in jail for the crime of being a Baptist rather than being honored as a hero of the faith.

Not only that, but if one reads Cotton Mather's famous volume *The Great Works of Christ in America*, published in 1702, it is more than evident that the spiritual zeal of New England's founding fathers had long departed. Mather knew that America was not the Christian city shining upon the hill that the early settlers dreamed of it as being.

In fact, this had in effect been conceded in 1662, the year before Mather was born, in the Half Way Covenant in Massachusetts, the original Puritan colony. The rulers realized, fifty years after it had begun, that fourth- and fifth-generation Americans were certainly not as clearly Christian as their illustrious ancestors, if indeed they were truly Christian at all.

As evangelicals, this is a question we must ponder carefully, and as a theologically very conservative British Calvinist (with Baptist tendencies) it is an area in which I have to tread *most* carefully, for I know that my views here will considerably color the views of many readers in relation to this whole book! Since this is also a political hot potato in the USA—something that is not the case in Britain, where culture war issues either do not exist or do not cross partisan boundaries—I know I need to be even more careful. But I do think that we cannot as evangelicals, especially those of Reformed persuasion like me, avoid it when we look at America's origins since it is still a matter of sharp debate today.

Through my mother's mother, Bethan Phillips (later Bethan Lloyd-Jones), I am something like seventh- or eighth-generation in a line of evangelical Christians stretching back in Wales to at least the eighteenth century—the period we are discussing—if not even earlier, into Puritan times. I thank God for so wonderful a continuous Christian heritage!

But does that make me a Christian? Biblically the answer is, most certainly not! That was the whole problem with the Jews in our Lord's lifetime. They thought that heredity or blood descent, combined with some good works, could get them into heaven. But as Christ told Nicodemus, unless you are *born again*—that is, born spiritually, not just physically—you cannot enter the Kingdom of Heaven. Being saved is an *individual* matter, and ancestry, however godly, plays no part. Think how many wonderfully Christian parents have godless children, and how many others are redeemed and truly saved from the most anti-Christian, wicked homes.

Not only that, but if we think of it from a Reformed (or as Bethan Lloyd-Jones would say, simply "biblical") viewpoint, this point is surely more powerful still. It is God who chooses us, not we ourselves. If we see the twenty-first-century world in which we live, we cannot but observe that today countries that were for centuries in darkness are now seeing converts by the tens of thousands, if not by the millions, and nations that once thought of themselves as Christian are increasingly turning their back not just on Christianity but on any kind of belief at all.

In other words, as the Puritans realized by the 1660s, and as Cotton Mather saw with much clarity in the 1690s and later, you cannot inherit Christian faith. Biblically that is impossible.

While writing this, my church in Cambridge was studying Jeremiah. Earlier generations of Judah had been godly, and as late as Josiah there was a ruler who truly loved the Lord. But in the end, by the time of Jeremiah, the moment of judgment had come, and the Jews were forced into exile in Babylon. When Christ came hundreds of years later, the majority of the Jews of His era did not recognize Him as God's long-promised Messiah.

What has changed today?

I would argue that biblically speaking nothing has changed at all.

I remember debating these crucial issues with the late Francis Schaeffer, one of the greatest evangelical giants of the twentieth century, a wonderful man whose prophetic voice speaks to us still (perhaps more than ever since his God-given insights speak so prophetically to the postmodern mush with which we find ourselves surrounded today, especially in his pivotal concept of *true truth*). Some of our correspondence is quoted in *The Great Evangelical Disaster*, with my name removed.

Schaeffer, like any true Reformed thinker, realized that Jesus is *both Savior and Lord* simultaneously and that it is simply cheap grace to regard Christ as the first but not the second. But on these issues I am closer to another, still alive American preacher, John F. MacArthur, who has also reminded us that Christ must be the Lord of our lives as well as our Savior. His book *Why Government Can't Save You* shows that you can be a conservative (and in MacArthur's case, now also Reformed), evangelical Christian and still be dubious as to what mere human government can achieve in terms of *spiritual* renewal.

Don't get me wrong—I agree fully with Schaeffer (and with my own father, Sir Fred Catherwood) in agreeing that God sets up governments, and that government per se, as Paul makes evident in Romans and Peter in his epistles, is of God and is designed by God. Therefore government is, by scriptural definition, a good thing, for God created it.

But the functions of a government, even one containing many godly people, and those of the church are quite different, and this is what I think has become confused in the minds of many evangelicals today.

Being of Reformed persuasion, I would hold strongly to the idea that since Christians are salt and light, God places us in society in order to do good. Not only that, but since "the earth is the LORD's" (Psalm 24:1), that includes all areas of life, not just the overtly spiritual. In saying all this, I agreed with Francis Schaeffer 200 percent, all the more so because at that time, back in the 1970s, he was one of the few evangelicals recalling us to our prophetic duty as God's people living in a secular world.

However, as time passed even Schaeffer began to look upon the "Christian past" of the USA with rose-tinted glasses, and as a historian and as a fellow-Calvinist evangelical I found this problematic.

Historically speaking, as much of what is now the USA was founded by godless men wanting to make money as it was by godly Puritans wanting to worship the Lord in freedom and truth. Secular America has deep seventeenth-century roots as much as its evangelical side. Not only that, but it soon became clear, even in those regions with Puritan origins, that Christian commitment is not and cannot be hereditary, if we understand the biblical doctrine of conversion properly.

We see this especially in a state such as Virginia, which was entirely commercial in origin and officially Anglican, often of a weak and not at all Puritan kind, especially since many of the Cavaliers (followers of King Charles I) who played such a key role in that colony were people who wanted to get away from Puritan-ruled England and opposed all that the Puritans believed in and stood for.

Being married to an American, I celebrate Thanksgiving every year, and my British parents usually celebrate in the USA with the man who introduced me to my wife, Crossway author and noted pastor, Mark Dever of Washington, D.C. However, as my wife Paulette discovered on visiting Plymouth, Massachusetts with her family as a child, some think that the current USA began there. This is quite false—the first American colony was Virginia, a secular foundation that began as a pure business venture.

So while it is natural for us as evangelicals to emphasize the Puritans—so many of whose views and values we share as deeply as ever today—it is historically quite inaccurate to see the origins of the USA through Puritan spectacles. When we talk—anachronistically it should be said—of reclaiming America, do we mean Puritan New England or Cavalier Virginia? Both, for good or ill, are equally America.

So, were many fine Christians involved in America's early days? Yes! Were there also numerous ungodly, greedy materialists in its infancy? Alas, we have to admit there were many of them too.

How about the eighteenth-century Founding Fathers—can we claim them? I think, as evangelical scholar Mark Noll has shown, the answer there is no too. *Some* of them might have been real Christians in the sense that we would understand it, but can we really say that Jefferson and Franklin, to take but two, were people we would recognize as clear evangelical Christians? I think not. Most of them were Deists, people who believed God set the world in motion and then left it to its own devices. While I want to say in the next chapter that even the Deists in the early USA were more influenced by seventeenth-century Puritan thinking on issues such as freedom and the rule of law and of democracy than they were by their French Enlightenment contemporaries, nonetheless I do not think we could claim the vast majority of them as fellow Christians.

Some colonies did allow greater degrees of freedom than, say, Massachusetts or Virginia. Pennsylvania, literally Penn's Wood, was founded by William Penn (1644–1718). Penn was a Quaker from a wealthy family who was expelled from Oxford for his faith. While the majority of that colony's inhabitants were soon no longer only Quakers—many of them were Mennonites from Central Europe, for example—religious freedom was a key component of Pennsylvania from its inception. Maryland was founded in honor of the Virgin Mary by the family of

Lord Baltimore, the Calverts. America's smallest state, Rhode Island, also enjoyed religious freedom, especially through one of its founders Roger Williams (c. 1604–1683). One of its earliest citizens was Obadiah Williams, a Baptist who in 1675 made it evident that not only should church and state be separate, but that as God chooses who is saved, the only members of the church should be the genuinely converted, something obvious today but a very radical view for the late seventeenth century, when church membership and citizenship were all too readily entangled.

In other words, we don't need to invent a mythic Golden Age in order to want our country to return to Christian values and true faith in Christ as Savior today.

Does America need a new Great Awakening? I hope the answer of all my readers is a resounding chorus of "Yes! Amen!"

When Jonathan Edwards and George Whitefield preached to thousands back in the eighteenth century, and tens of thousands were born again as real Christians, was that a government-sponsored event? No; it was the work of the Holy Spirit in redemption, bringing countless numbers of men and women to salvation in Jesus as Savior.

I am one of a whole generation of evangelical Christians whose formative years in the 1960s and 1970s were totally transformed by the writing and thinking of Francis Schaeffer (and in my case a powerful infusion from Dr. D. Martyn Lloyd-Jones, his friend and contemporary). God still calls His people to be salt and light in society, and that includes Christians going into the professions, the arts and sciences, and that God-ordained institution of government as well.

But as John MacArthur would remind us, who or what *saves* you?

Actually, in what he told me and wrote himself, Francis Schaeffer provided the biblical answer from the Scriptures.

Take the issue of abortion, perhaps *the* major issue that has led so many evangelicals to become politically active and involved.

As Schaeffer once said to me, the *real* problem is not so much abortion as the *abortion mentality*. This is in fact a classic chicken and egg problem! Why do so many abortions happen? Surely, as Schaeffer pointed out, the *real* reason is that people don't see it as morally wrong. For the average person today it is not murder but a simple surgical procedure. But it is a spiritual issue more than a legal one. The eyes of the ordinary Briton or American are blind, and they fail to see that what they think of as normal is in fact sin.

As evangelicals, as Christians who believe the Bible, we know that *ultimately* all problems are spiritual in root. I am a teetotaler; so I have many sympathies with those well-meaning Prohibitionists in the USA who made alcohol illegal for a brief period in the twentieth century but who failed completely in their well-intentioned task.

Suppose there really was a third (or some would like to say, fourth) Great Awakening in the USA. Would the abortion rate go down? You can be sure of it! Not only that, but since abortion is usually performed on unmarried women who have had pre- or extramarital sex, the need to have abortions would also plummet since the cause of abortions would diminish drastically.

For British evangelicals, this is the Oliver Cromwell issue. Cromwell, during his period in power, experimented with having Christian-only Parliaments and did all he could to legislate Christian morality into law. But when he died in 1658 his regime lasted just two more years, and when King Charles II came to the throne, Britain had one of its most immoral periods in history, the Restoration. Britain could not have had godlier rulers than in the Commonwealth and Protectorate (1649–1660), and it is also the case that no king was ever successful in reintroducing despotic government. This was because of the freedoms Cromwell was able to achieve for the British people. Politically Cromwell's legacy has thus been permanent. But most British citizens were not the Christians that their leaders were, and after 1660 that showed. Bunyan's portrait of Vanity Fair is an accurate portrayal of the Restoration period.

Does this have lessons for us today?

I think it does. It shows that activism only brings in limited results, and what truly makes the difference is *spiritual* change, people being born again. If a young woman is a Christian, and practices godly Christian morality, she will not get illicitly pregnant and so will not need an abortion. The abortion rate will plummet because those who would have had them in the past will not get pregnant in the first place. Such change does not need an alteration in the law. The *inward* change that Locke spoke of and that is at the heart of the gospel message will have made all the difference.

Of course, that does not preclude the kind of Christian salt and light action in the public square (to use Richard John Neuhaus's expression) that Reformed Christians such as Schaeffer (and Calvin before him) have never ceased to advocate. But it does suggest that social action—including in fields such as the arts and sciences, where the number of Christians is growing—is not enough on its own. We need evangelism and action to go hand in hand.

In my book *Whose Side Is God on?* I have dealt in more detail with the issue of whether we can say that colonial America was a Christian country. Sadly, this debate seems to have become politicized, and as a British evangelical writing about another country's history, that is something I wish to avoid. But whatever the historic merits of each side, I think we can all agree that the USA is a very secular place *today*, albeit with a far higher percentage of active, practicing Christians than in any other part of the secular West.

This is why I tend to be optimistic when I look at the USA. From a British perspective, far more Americans are Christian than in, say, Britain, whereas many American evangelicals I know are pessimistic, concentrating instead on how secular the culture has become!

So rather than debating what proportion of the Founding Fathers really were Christians in the sense that we would understand that now, is it not better for us as evangelicals to be active salt and light for our own day, the time in which God has placed us, and to do all possible to be faithful witnesses to the culture around us of the good news of Jesus Christ? We can learn from the mistakes of the Puritans as well as from their good side and see how we can achieve a biblical balance of gospel and action for our own circumstances.

As we shall see, some historians believe that the Methodist Revival in Britain stopped that country from having the kind of overtly anti-Christian, violent revolution of the sort that happened in France in 1689. I think that such a case certainly has merit, even if it is not the entire story. But if thousands turn to Christ in conversion, the change in their lives is both inward and permanent, *real* change, with sinners becoming new creations in Jesus. Some Christians, alas, even today think that evangelism and social action are incompatible. To me they go hand in hand, as the message of the New Testament makes clear. I think this is what the lesson of the seventeenth century is to us today in the twenty-first: Jesus is Savior and Lord, and we must always proclaim him as both.

Puritans and Separatists

These two groups of Protestant Christians are often confused with each other. It is important that we realize the difference since their descendants remain so today, especially in the USA, with some Christians wanting to make a godly impression on the surrounding culture, and others wishing to retreat from it into a Christian enclave.

The *Puritans* had a strong sense of being God's covenant people here on earth. As a result they saw the colonies they created as God's Promised Land where they could start life anew, away from the horrors of the Old World.

This sense of America being a special nation has persisted, even now that most Americans do not share the faith of the original Massachusetts settlers. It is perhaps significant that one of the most highly regarded recent books on American foreign policy, by churchgoing University of Pennsylvania professor Walter McDougall, is entitled *Promised Land, Crusader State*, with *Crusader* here being used benignly, not in its eleventh-century sense.

American concepts such as *Manifest Destiny* (which came into being in the nineteenth century) or the *American Dream*, of more recent vintage, are all current embodiments, in a secularized way, of the original concept of the American colonies being bright cities shining upon a hill, a term that itself comes straight from Scripture. Even though most Americans today are secular, this sense of optimism still prevails, regardless of political affiliation, and while it has been described as American Exceptionalism and has been misunderstood in recent years by non-Americans, there is still a refreshing wholesomeness to the USA that always strikes visitors from a more cynical Europe as a highly positive feature of contemporary American society.

The key thing to remember also is that in Britain (and in, for example, the Palatinate or the Pfalz region of Germany), the Puritans and their devout Continental European equivalents were mainly people who for decades wanted to stay *within* the Established Church in the hope of reforming or purifying it. Historians have demonstrated that while, for example, Queen Elizabeth I was no Puritan, many eminent churchmen in England were, certainly as far down as the mass expulsion in 1662.

Under the Stuarts, though, the Puritans, while within, were under increasing pressure, especially when Laud was appointed Archbishop of Canterbury, Laud being an avowed ritualist and Arminian. The leadership of the Church of England became increasingly Catholic ritually while being careful to remain Protestant politically.

Needless to say, this was ever more unacceptable to the large numbers of grass-roots Puritans within the church. It was from such people that the Puritan emigration to America came.

However, although they were deeply unhappy with the doctrinal drift of the Church of England, it is important to remember that they were *not* against a state church per se. (This is where I have to declare an interest and say that while I am Reformed in doctrine, my view of church and state is Baptist, despite being on the leadership team of an evangelical/Reformed/Believer Baptist Church of England Church!) Therefore, when the Puritans arrived in the New World, they did not grant religious freedom to those whose views differed doctrinally from their own.

We tend, and with good cause, to remember all the good and wonderful things about the Puritans. And we should, since spiritually they have so much to teach us, and one can also add that so much of what is very positive about the USA today is derived in enormous measure from America's Puritan heritage.

But, alas, the Puritans were highly intolerant of those who disagreed with them, and here we should surely beg to diverge from what they believed and how they chose to enforce those views.

These were not just on moral issues, such as portrayed in Hawthorne's famous novel *The Scarlet Letter*. Far worse was a series of real-life events. Between 1659 and 1661 four leading Quakers were executed for no other reason than their different interpretation of the Christian faith. King Charles II was so horrified that he had to intervene as king to prevent more executions from taking place—even though Bunyan might have been jailed during his reign, he was at least not put to death.

So we now need to look at the other group, the *Separatists*.

Such groups, or denominations as we would now describe them, as the Baptists and Quakers would best be described as separatists since they did not believe that state and church should be united in any way. As we saw, this meant reverting to the pattern of the early church, to Christianity before Constantine.

For Americans, it is important to remember that the official constitutional separation of church and state comes not from the Puritans but from the separatists and their influence upon the Bill of Rights in which such freedom is enshrined legally.

As we shall see, it was the separatists who were the great spiritual beneficiaries of the Great Awakening in the USA. It was separatist denominations—especially Baptists, Methodists (who were new at that time), and similar groups—that grew exponentially as a result of that wonderful work of God rather than the older denominations of Puritan heritage.

Now the USA is one of the most diverse places on earth, with many Protestant denominations unique to that country. A nineteenth-century French writer, Alexis de Tocqueville, noted in traveling around the infant USA that religious freedom there actually helped Christian faith since, unlike back in Europe, no one form of Christianity was linked to an oppressive state. When one looks at the enormous comparative strength of American Christianity as opposed to the increasingly moribund state of affairs in European countries that still have state churches (such as England, Scotland, and Denmark), one can see what he meant. While doctrinally I might feel much closer to the Puritans, the separatists also had a strong case, and I would argue that they ultimately benefited American Christianity in the long run.

The Origin of the Baptists

It was always a source of great joy to my late father-in-law, John S. Moore, a lifelong and faithful Baptist pastor, that the Baptists in the USA became in his lifetime the single biggest Protestant grouping in America. Now that it is once again becoming evangelical theologically (and through exceptionally gifted leaders such as Crossway author Mark Dever is rediscovering its Reformed doctrinal roots), this is surely significant.

How did the Baptists begin?

Here historians do not all agree since some see links to the German Anabaptists, whom we saw earlier, in the sixteenth century and others place their origins quite separately, in England a hundred or so years later, in the seventeenth century.

I am opting in this book for the latter interpretation.

The English Puritan John Smyth (who died in 1612) became a separatist and fled to the Netherlands, where he baptized himself in 1608. He, like others, sought to create a pure church, one consisting of believers only. He came to feel that baptism, therefore, should also be for believers alone, since he believed, as have Baptists ever since, that this is the correct biblical pattern.

His fellow Baptist was Thomas Helwys (c. 1550–1616). Helwys led a group back to England, where they formed the first ever General Baptist Church in London in 1612.

Baptists at that time included both Calvinists (known then as Particular Baptists, nowadays Grace Baptists) and Arminians (who were called General Baptists). By the restoration of King Charles II in 1660 England had around three hundred individual Baptist congregations. During the Commonwealth and Protectorate many Baptists achieved leading positions, including service as officers in the New Model Army, the Puritan army led by Cromwell that had overthrown King Charles I.

But as we have seen, 1660–1689 was a period of acute persecution. Baptists, as true separatists, completely rejected the notion of a state church, quite apart from their theological rejection of the Anglican doctrine of baptizing infants. Not only that but the restored Royalists wanted revenge on anyone who had supported the Parliamentary side in the Civil War.

With the passing of the Act of Toleration in 1689, Baptists benefited from newfound freedom for nonconformist Protestants. Sadly, some Baptists went doctrinally astray and denied the Trinity—these are the ancestors of today's Unitarians.

Today Baptists are some of the most significant of all Christian denominations, and beyond that, many other groups insist on baptism of believers only, although they would not claim to be Baptist denominationally. What began with a flight to the Netherlands of one man now has huge spiritual significance around the world.

SEVEN

Awakening and Evangelicals

In the period we will examine in this chapter, God worked in amazing ways. But first we must set the scene.

A Background to the Eighteenth Century

We now call ourselves evangelicals, Christians who believe in the *evangel*, the good news of Jesus Christ. Strictly speaking, although at the heart of the historical, biblical tradition of Christianity, this word mainly stems from its use in the eighteenth century. Two major events happened during this hundred-year period, and they could not be more unalike. One was the Great Awakening, in which countless men and women found life in Christ, both in North America and through its British equivalent, the Methodist Revival in the United Kingdom. The other event was the Enlightenment, a philosophical movement that would by the end of the eighteenth century turn many against religious faith of any kind and lead to the gruesome French Revolution, in which thousands were put to death for their political beliefs in an orgy of massacre and counter-massacre.

Today, in the twenty-first century, we are supposedly living in a postmodern or post-enlightenment era. Since postmodernism is notoriously difficult to define, it is hard even to know if this claim is true. Since the French Revolution in 1789 and the fall of the Communist Iron Curtain in 1989, some talk about two hundred years of modernity. However, these people tend to be sociologists or political scientists, not historians. Many of the ideas of the Enlightenment had been around for a very long time by 1789, and Tsarina Catherine the Great of Russia, a despot, was as much a disciple and friend of the French philosopher Voltaire as were his numerous radical followers in revolutionary France.

Not only that, but in science the real revolution was in Britain, not France, and many of the leaders of the scientific revolution—what some have called the British Enlightenment—were keen Christians (for example, Robert Boyle and John Wilkins, not to forget professing Christians such as the more famous Sir Isaac Newton).

Finally, I think it fair to say that the American Revolution of 1776 was innately different from the far more violent version in France thirteen years later. While I do not go along with attempts to baptize the Founding Fathers, nevertheless it is true that what many call the Second Great Awakening took place in the infant USA in a way that would have been inconceivable in a nation as secular as France.

The USA, however deistic the beliefs of most of its founders, owed far more ideologically to the Glorious Revolution of 1689 in Britain and its concepts of liberty derived from the Puritan Commonwealth and Protectorate in England than it did from the avowedly antireligious sentiments of the European Enlightenment. So while in the last chapter I stressed we must not overdo the Christian heritage of the West, here I would want to emphasize that we should not neglect it either.

The Great Awakening

As we saw, many godly Americans realized that the Colonies had lost their spiritual roots—those, of course, that had ever had them, as many of the settlements were commercial and secular in origin, not Puritan. Cotton Mather had seen this as early as 1702, and probably long before.

By the 1730s the spiritual state of the New World colonies was worse still. Then from 1733 onward, all this began to change in a most wonderful way. An intellectual named Jonathan Edwards (1703–1758), who had been educated at Yale, began to preach a series of sermons that turned North America upside down. His preaching launched what we now call the Great Awakening and what is also called, in theological parlance, a revival. As Edwards himself put it, "souls did as it were come by floods to Jesus Christ." Thousands were converted and lives transformed. Edwards, in writing about it afterward, tells us:

> There was scarcely a single person in the town, old or young, left unconcerned about the great things of the eternal world. . . . This work of God, as it was carried out, and the number of true saints multiplied, soon made a glorious alteration in the town; so that in Spring and Summer following, *anno* 1735, the town seemed to be full of the presence of God.

Similar tales were told of the Welsh Revival in Britain in 1904–1905, where the crime rate plummeted, for example, as people hitherto dishonest were converted and became new creations in Christ.

Another tremendous influence during this time was a British preacher, an Oxford graduate named George Whitefield (1714–1770). He arrived in the colonies in 1740 and was soon addressing crowds of over twenty thousand people. Soon all thirteen of the Colonies were under the Awakening's sway.

The Awakening Comes to Britain

Now the Awakening was to cross the Atlantic. In Britain it is usually called the Methodist Revival, and with good cause, since the Wesley brothers, John and Charles, were integral to it. But Whitefield played a vital part himself, and he was what we would describe as a Calvinistic Methodist, an unusual combination then and since and not well known outside of Wales, although the founding Calvinistic Methodists, such as Whitefield and Selina, Countess of Huntington, were English. But we should not ignore two great Welshmen—Daniel Rowland (1713–1790) of Llangeitho (a town later closely associated with another Welsh spiritual giant, D. Martyn Lloyd-Jones) and Howell Harris (1714–1773).

What this shows is that both Calvinists and Arminians played a critical role in the Revival, and that to ignore the former because of the larger fame of the latter is to gain a false perspective on what happened.

Strangely Warmed: The Origins and Impact of Methodism

John Wesley (1703–1791) and his brother Charles (1707–1788) started off as High Church (= ritualistic) Anglicans. At Oxford they established a club for holy living, and the word *Methodist* was originally used as an insult to describe the methods they employed to live righteous lives under their own effort.

Everything changed when the brothers met some Moravian missionaries in London. The Moravians were the spiritual descendants of the earlier Mennonites and were making a major impact upon many in the capital. In 1738 both John and Charles Wesley had remarkable spiritual experiences. John was to describe his as being "strangely warmed" after hearing someone read Luther's book on the epistle to the Romans.

Just over eighteen months later a larger gathering, this time including Whitefield, had another experience of the Holy Spirit, with everyone,

Wesley later recalled, all singing together the words, "We praise Thee, O God, we acknowledge Thee to be the Lord."

Soon thereafter both George Whitefield and John Wesley were traveling the length and breadth of Britain, preaching to enormous crowds, multitudes of whom became Christians as a result. Over the next fifty years, it is reckoned, Wesley alone traveled over 250,000 miles, mostly on horseback, in an age in which travel over any distance was hard. Wesley was also a prolific author, pamphleteer, and editor of a theological journal.

We will look shortly at what revival is and means. Here we will look at the rise of Methodism, now a denomination in decline, but for a long while one of the most vibrant parts of Protestantism worldwide.

It is important to note that both Wesley brothers technically died Anglicans—members of the Church of England. Methodism was not separatist by choice, and it did not become an officially separate denomination until after John's death in 1791. Even as late as the 1960s there were still discussions about Methodism, at least in Britain, being reincorporated back into the Anglican fold.

It was the spiritually dead hierarchy of the Established Church, most of whom were political appointees, who looked down their long noses at what they decried as Methodist "enthusiasm." (Lord Melbourne, a later British Prime Minister, said that things had come to a pretty pass if religion was going to start becoming personal.) One angry aristocrat wrote to the godly Selina, Countess of Huntington, who introduced Whitefield and others to court circles, to tell her that she did not like being described as a sinner.

In effect, therefore, Methodism began as a subset of the Church of England, unlike the much smaller denomination, the Countess of Huntington's Connexion (the Calvinistic Methodists), and initially existed as a safe spiritual home for the tens of thousands converted through Wesley's itinerant ministry. John Wesley drew up the rules in 1743, Methodism was recognized under the Toleration Act in 1787, and three years earlier Wesley had sent Francis Asbury to the infant

United States to establish Methodist missionary activity on the other side of the Atlantic.

As John Wesley put it, "Justification by faith is the doctrine of the Church as well as of the Bible." Methodists also put large stress on holiness, something that was to lead indirectly to Pentecostalism and its holiness teaching in the twentieth century. If one includes modern Pentecostalism as a descendant of the original Methodism, then the Methodists can claim to be truly global today, even if the actual denomination is no longer what it once was.

The social impact of Methodism has been enormous, especially in Britain. A French historian, Halevy, once claimed that the Methodist Revival prevented Britain from having a violent revolution (remember that Wesley's later years were those of the bloodthirsty and exceptionally anti-religious French Revolution). There is something to be said for this, but I also think that the thought of John Locke and the comparatively bloodless Glorious Revolution of 1688–1689 in Britain also helped since, whatever we might think of the disastrous policies of King George III, he was no absolutist despot.

Be that as it may, many ordinary working-class Britons—people whose peasant and artisan equivalents in France were active revolutionaries—became Christians through the Revival, putting their hope in something far more important as a result.

Consequently although many of them espoused radical politics, it was not of the killing kind. Early trade unionists were often Methodists, and so were many of the more benign factory owners, who took seriously what the Bible says on how to treat your employees. Christians, as we shall see later on, were at the heart of benevolent social change and improvement in Britain, in the same way that many Christians in the USA actively worked for freedom for slaves. In fact, right up until the 1970s many leading Labour politicians were also Methodist lay preachers, causing the joke to be made that the Labour Party was "more Methodism than Marx."

Indeed, the Labour Party was itself founded by an evangelical, Keir Hardie, and there are evangelicals in leading positions in all the major British political parties, Labour included, down to this day.

Remember, while the hierarchy of the Church of England was often fairly godless, large numbers of biblical Christians remained in it at the grass roots then as now.

We still sing the hymns of one of them—John Newton, the former slave trader who was wondrously born again and whose hymn "Amazing Grace" is as popular now as it was then. William Grimshaw and Henry Venn both proved that while bishops may forget the truth, ordinary parishes are transformed through the power of the gospel.

Above all, the fact that hundreds of thousands of evangelical university and college students worldwide are today in Christian ministry groups on campus, whether the International Fellowship of Evangelical Students or denominational organizations such as RUF, is all ultimately owed to one faithful preacher in Cambridge, Charles Simeon. Simeon preached for decades during this period at his parish church, Holy Trinity, with a powerful ministry to university students there.

This led after his death to the still flourishing Cambridge Inter-Collegiate Christian Union, which in its turn led to similar evangelical student ministries first in Britain and then globally.

The Protestants Catch Up: The Dawn of the Great Century

The nineteenth century is often nicknamed "the Great Century" by writers discussing mission, and with good cause since it was then that the church really did finally, albeit eighteen hundred years late, fulfill Christ's command to take the gospel to all the nations. But the decisions that enabled such a spiritually profitable work began in the eighteenth century.

In 1792 the Baptist Missionary Society was founded, its most famous member being William Carey, who went to India. The London Missionary Society began in 1795, and this was significant in that it was interdenominational, something we are quite used to today but was then quite a striking innovation. The Church of England's own group, the Church Missionary Society, started in 1799. By 1804 the Methodists were active in dispatching missionaries of their own. That year also saw the foundation of the British and Foreign Bible Society, which still exists and is today active in promoting the Scriptures through evangelically sound Bible translations such as the *English Standard Version*.

Except for the now-defunct London Missionary Society (LMS), the work of eighteenth-century missionary societies continues, albeit in different form. Increasingly the sending countries for such missions are now well beyond the West. I have heard of Latvian missionaries, for example, Latvia being a country long under Russian and then Soviet oppression, coming to evangelize non-Christian West Europeans. Many Nigerian and Peruvian evangelicals are to be found as missionaries to secular Britain, and one can think of many similar examples. Secondly, Westerners in Two-Thirds World countries go not to tell local Christians what to do but to act as mission partners, supporting the work of the often thriving indigenous churches. The world of mission continues more strongly than ever before, but in new and exciting ways.

The Cult of Enlightenment and the Two Revolutions

We looked earlier at the Enlightenment. In many European countries—democratic and officially tolerant Britain thankfully an exception—Christianity was associated with repressive governments and a despotic, often deeply corrupt papacy. As a result many intellectuals rejected religion altogether, even though some philosophers, such as Voltaire, had friendly correspondence with those monarchs given the surely self-contradictory nickname of "Enlightened Despots," such as Frederick the Great of Prussia (a country now divided between Germany and Poland) and Catherine the Great of Russia.

Come the French Revolution of 1789, therefore, not only were thousands of aristocrats massacred, but so too were ordinary church-men and in due time many of the original revolutionaries themselves. As the old saying goes, the revolution always devours its own children. Look too at the Stalinist purges and Red Terror in the USSR after 1917. The Catholic Church was violently disestablished, and Robespierre, one of the early revolutionary leaders, went so far as to establish a neo-pagan "Cult of the Supreme Being" in the place of Christianity.

Eventually, as often happens, a strong man took over to reimpose order on all the chaos. This was Napoleon, who ironically crowned himself as emperor, with the Pope in the audience.

Napoleon allowed Catholicism to flourish again. But he also legal-ized Protestantism—a not insignificant number of French Protestants had survived despite all the persecution—and also Judaism, ending centuries of anti-Semitism in France. This was good news, but the legacy he left in much of Europe was an aggressive secularism, which is still strong in France, with separation of church and state remaining the official creed of that country to this day. Much of Europe is the most secular part of the world, impervious to the gospel, and not so much nominally Catholic as really nothing at all.

The American Alternative

It is interesting that America, which also had a revolution in the eigh-teenth century, is very much the opposite. Up until recently, Harvard professor Harvey Cox and his secularization theory was all the rage in academic circles. Now even sociologists of religion, ironically not usually the most sympathetic people to their subject, have awakened to the fact that the world is in reality now moving swiftly in precisely the opposite direction—toward becoming *more* religious, rather than reli-gion fading as the world becomes more technologically advanced.

For those interested in the literature on this, books by Boston profes-sor Peter Bergen are fascinating, as are those by French specialist Gilles

Kepel, whose international bestseller from the 1990s, *The Revenge of God*, awakened many secular thinkers to what was happening all around them.

Therefore, as non-religious academics found themselves forced to realize, it is *they* who are today the global exception rather than the rule. In fact, it is western Europe (and, one could perhaps add, the religion and sociology departments of major American universities) that are still secular, while the rest of the world is more religious than ever before. From a Christian viewpoint not all of this is good news—a Marxist sociologist and a Muslim imam are equally anti-Christian, although the former would be secular and the latter very definitely religious.

But to me at least the fact that the world's most technologically advanced and modern country, the USA, is also profoundly religious and has a growing Christian minority is surely a cause for rejoicing.

The Second Great Awakening

By the beginning of the nineteenth century the effects of the original Great Awakening were wearing off. Not only that but the denominational structure of the infant American Republic was changing—new or different denominations were taking over from the Congregationalists and Episcopalians (the latter now being independent from England), especially Baptists and Methodists, the latter, of course, being an entirely recent creation.

Some have called the continual phenomenal growth of Christian faith, especially in the 1820s and 1830s, a Second Great Awakening, and this is as good a name as any.

Secular historians have pointed to the incomparable Jonathan Edwards and suggested that no one matched him in the nineteenth century. This is perhaps unfair, though one could say that no one was able to combine his theological genius with a simultaneous and indisputable anointing from God in the power of his preaching and evangelism.

However, Charles Hodge (1797–1878) at Princeton could, I would argue, come close on theological exposition and the defense of the gospel. In that era Liberalism, if one can call it that so early on, was creeping into what had been evangelical territory, in terms of what is described as the New School, based around Nathaniel William Taylor at Yale and, more dangerously, overt Unitarianism in the teaching of Horace Bushnell. Taylor opposed both Calvinist orthodoxy and Unitarianism and doubted the biblical doctrine of original sin, a view that has historically been called Pelagianism.

It was therefore important that Reformed evangelical theology had a mighty defender in Charles Hodge, who throughout his long academic career stuck firmly by what he knew to be biblical truths. After 1846 Hodge also strongly opposed slavery, as we shall see in the next chapter. As once orthodox places such as Harvard fell to error—appointing a Unitarian to a key post as early as 1805—Hodge realized that the support of historically accurate theology was not just a mere academic exercise but the defense of truth itself.

Also of concern to Hodge was the new method of evangelism being put forward by Charles Finney (1792–1875). Here I need to be cautious, since many an evangelical today remains a fervent admirer of Finney, and there is no question that his main evangelistic efforts, in the so-called "Burned-Over" region of New York in the 1820s and 1830s, were very fruitful, with thousands being converted. But Hodge was perturbed by Finney's strongly Arminian theology and by the human methodology his New Measures in evangelism clearly espoused.

Significantly Nathaniel William Taylor, a Pelagian, strongly supported Finney and disliked the fact that Reformed theologians such as Hodge dared to criticize Finney at all. Here is an interesting theological question: in the eighteenth century God blessed the Calvinist Whitefield and the Arminian Wesley and has indeed blessed Calvinist and Arminian evangelism ever since, even though, as classics such as J. I. Packer's *Evangelism and the Sovereignty of God* demonstrate, Calvinists have a much more solid biblical basis for their evangelism. What does this tell us?

I think what worries me about Finney and those of his ilk since is that pragmatism came to be the norm. Finney has certainly been the role model for generations of evangelists since the 1830s right down to Billy Graham in our own time. Evangelistic methods such as asking people to come forward as inquirers all date from Finney's time. Finney retired to a pastorate and then to a highly influential presidency at Oberlin College in Ohio.

Here one should add that Graham has, unlike Finney, always worked closely with local evangelical churches, whereas Finney would barnstorm into a town without any prior consultation.

This era also saw many campfire meetings in woods and other outdoor venues, often charged with emotion, with famous gatherings at places such as Gasper River and Cane Ridge in 1801. These, historians have suggested, are proof of the democratic nature of America influencing its theology. Many of the leaders of such meetings were not highly theologically trained but were able to speak to ordinary folk in a language that the average man or woman could clearly understand.

All this came as the infant Republic moved toward genuine religious freedom, starting with Jefferson's Virginia in 1786. Although Jefferson was no Christian, he understood, as Locke had before him, that conversion and spiritual belief was not something that the state could enforce, as it needed to come sincerely from within. Virginia, having persecuted non-Anglicans, now paved the way for the religious freedom that the rest of the USA was to go on to enjoy. The First Amendment to the Constitution, in the Bill of Rights, guaranteed religious freedom for all Americans. Here one should not forget that states like Massachusetts did not grant local state religious freedom until 1833, but at least no denominational version of Christianity was imposed by government decree on ordinary citizens, in line with the original intent behind the First Amendment.

The guarantee of that Amendment did not intend to abolish Christianity from the public sphere altogether—something that Christian legal authorities today such as Sam Ericsson have not hesitated to remind us. The theologically liberal/secular humanist interpretation of the Amendment is historically entirely inaccurate, as evangelicals today correctly point out.

Ralph Waldo Emerson (1803–1882) and Joseph Smith (1805–1844) are two, albeit very different, symptoms of what was going wrong at the same time as many a revival was breaking out in the Second Great Awakening.

Emerson, now revered as an illustrious American poet, was also a Unitarian, though he came from an evangelical background. God became impersonal to him, and he is best known for his poetry on Transcendentalism, the idea that we can know the reality of the physical world through intuition.

In the mainstream secular world today, his views would be unexceptional, especially in the current postmodern climate, in which absolute knowledge is deemed to be impossible. But at the time they caused a shock—notably his lecture at Harvard early in his career when he denied Christ's divinity.

Joseph Smith was the founder of Mormonism, the first of the unusual religious views to be invented in North America. Strictly speaking the movement is called the Church of Jesus Christ of Latter Day Saints, though since it invented nonexistent golden tablets purportedly from God, the actual resemblance to genuine Christianity is fairly nonexistent. As Lawrence Foster has put it, the Book of Mormon, the basis of the religion, "is a highly complex work of the religious imagination."

Smith himself was murdered, and after various wanderings the Mormons ended up in Utah, especially Salt Lake City, which they dominate to this day. While Mormons tend to be moral and clean-cut, their theology, including their notorious acceptance of polygamy (technically abandoned in 1890 but still practiced by some), shows clearly that they are a false religion by biblical standards. By now they have moved well beyond their Utah base, with at least five million adherents worldwide.

Dispensationalism—New Theories or Old Truths?

It is with much trepidation that I mention another nineteenth-century development in American religion—Dispensationalism, an idea that in fact originated in Britain with J. N. Darby (1800–1882), a member of the Plymouth Brethren, who, like more recent denominations such as the twentieth-century Assemblies of God, hold to a dispensational view of Scripture as part of their core statement of faith. The view was further reinforced by the appearance of the Scofield Bible in 1909, which in slightly different form remains in print today.

The idea that sacred history is divided into separate dispensations—usually seven but sometimes more—is at the heart of dispensationalist teaching. We are, according to this view, now living in a church dispensation, at the end of which will come the Rapture when Christians are taken up into heaven and then the Second Coming of Christ. Dispensationalists also believe in what is called the premillennial version of the end times, and this in turn is divided into three schools of thought—pre-, mid-, and post-Tribulation, depending upon when the person believes the Rapture will occur and whether or not Christians will experience any of the Tribulation.

For much of church history, evangelicals have not believed in any of these interpretations. They have been either amillennial or, like the Puritans (and Charles Finney who would otherwise have differed strongly with that group), postmillennial.

However, many evangelicals today, especially in Pentecostal and Brethren circles, are strongly premillennialist and dispensationalist in their theology, and in the case of several well-known evangelical seminaries in the USA it is compulsory for faculty to be premillennial as part of being evangelical. This to me is a shame as it divides evangelicals on issues of eschatology—the precise details of the Second Coming—when all of us are united on the more important and spiritually crucial doctrine of soteriology, the nature of Christ's accomplishment and finished work in salvation upon the cross. One would hope that such divisions shall in time become a thing of the past, as it is a shame that genuine biblical evangelicals differ from one another on an issue that has divided equally godly Christians for centuries past. Baptist evangelicals recognize Presbyterian evangelicals as fellow evangelicals, for example, even though their differences on the nature of Christian baptism are centuries old.

Whitefield and Edwards

While many twentieth-century evangelicals in Reformed circles stated that they looked back to the Puritans for their prime historical inspiration, J. I. Packer was quite right when he said that the greatest of the Reformed preachers of that era, Dr. D. Martyn Lloyd-Jones, was "an eighteenth-century man." Lloyd-Jones was always careful to refer to himself as a "Bible Calvinist" rather than a "system Calvinist," and his insistence on the primacy of Scripture rather than on a favorite theologian of the past was a necessary warning to those of us in the Reformed wing of Evangelicalism to be Bible- rather than man-centered. Nonetheless, there is considerable merit in Packer's description of the Doctor, who also added Daniel Rowland and Howell Harris to his list of eighteenth-century heroes. But above all Lloyd-Jones revered both Whitefield and Edwards, and his personal copy of a portrait of Whitefield evangelizing ordinary working men and women in the fields is yards away from me as I write this.

Whitefield, that towering giant of evangelism, is equally well-known on both sides of the Atlantic, Edwards more so in the USA than in Britain (which is a shame).

Both are special because they were more than mighty evangelists used by God. What makes them remarkable is that they were profound intellects—educated at Oxford and Yale respectively—who had an enormous and lasting impact on listeners with no or very little education. They were thoughtful preachers whose sermons had an astonishing emotional impact on their audiences. This is what their twentieth-century follower Martyn Lloyd-Jones so aptly described as "logic on fire," a combination that is now all too rare and that we as evangelicals ought to rediscover.

The other special feature of these two men is that they believed fully in what has become known as the *doctrines of grace*. Nowadays we would call them Calvinists or Reformed. Both of them prove that the notion that those who believe in what the Bible teaches about the sovereign grace of God are not evangelistic is sheer nonsense, as we also saw when looking at the pivotal role that Geneva missionaries to France played in Calvin's own lifetime. The two Wesleys, by contrast, were Arminian, taking their cue from Arminius, a Dutch thinker. Because of the Wesleys' astonishing record in evangelism during the Methodist Revival and the equally important role of Whitefield and Wesley, it is all too easy to forget those who followed Calvin's (and one can also add Augustine's) interpretation of the Bible.

Whitefield is also interesting in that his career highlights that of a faithful aristocratic British woman, Selina, Countess of Huntington. She was an active personal evangelist herself and is the only woman ever to have founded a denomination, one that still exists, albeit in a different form, in Wales. Also, the Calvinistic Methodists were said to combine the fire of Methodism with the logic of Calvin, and that mix was certainly true of the Welsh preacher mentioned earlier, Martyn Lloyd-Jones.

Edwards is still revered in the USA, with major new biographies of him continuing to appear in recent years and a residential college named after him at his alma mater, Yale University. Even secular scholars in America revere him for his towering intellect, while rejecting the truth of his spiritual message.

When the first edition of this book appeared, Edwards was back in the news again because he had been taken up as a mascot by several charismatic groups, principally in the USA but also to a lesser extent in Britain. This is because of the remarkable physical phenomena accompanying many of his meetings, at which people under conviction of sin would wail, cry aloud, and do similar things.

Since I returned to academic life and left interdenominational evangelical Christian publishing as a career, I no longer meet people from so wide a spectrum. So I do not know whether such phenomena are as widespread now as they were a few years ago when enthusiastic Pentecostals likened the meetings of Jonathan Edwards with those of twentieth-century leaders such as the late John Wimber, at whose gatherings similar phenomena were also widespread. Either way we ought always to be careful to be Christ-centered, Scripture-inspired, and especially concerned not to believe things merely because they look spectacular or unusual.

But it is worth saying that Edwards was himself very aware in his own lifetime of the dangers that such phenomena could present. Much of his writing deals with how to separate the counterfeit from the genuine since he knew that ecstatic events could be psychologically induced or worse.

Having said that, Edwards was also unafraid of the emotional—the fiery side of logic on fire, if you like. This too is something that those of us on the Reformed side of the evangelical spectrum should not forget. It is perfectly possible to feel the truth as well as to know it, and while feelings can be highly misleading, we are God-created creatures with emotions as well as brains. Men such as Edwards and Whitefield showed that it is entirely possible to express emotion in combination with a thoroughly biblical doctrinal orthodoxy.

Revival

Revival in the classic meaning of the term, as historically understood, is a massive or unusual outpouring of the Holy Spirit upon the church. Not only do especially large numbers of non-Christians become converted, but the existing churches in a particular place are also revitalized.

However, in some parts of the USA revival means simply an evangelistic meeting. My late father-in-law would "conduct revivals," and a local church would announce that a "revival will take place at 10:30 A.M. next Sunday morning." Being British I found this use slightly difficult to absorb, though it is the description that many American readers would understand. So my employment of the term is the classic/British one—a special work of the Holy Spirit in conversion and church maturity.

The Great Awakening in Colonial America and the Methodist Revival in Britain, two famous eighteenth-century events, are excellent examples of revivals. Many would give a similar name to the remarkable conversions in Wales 1904–1906, with which many of my own Welsh ancestors were closely involved. Similar events have taken place in the areas in which Christianity expanded most in the twentieth century, such as in East Africa and in more recent times in Borneo in southeast Asia.

Christians have always longed for revival, and one of the major debates on this topic is whether it is a purely sovereign act of a gracious Heavenly Father or whether we can somehow encourage God along in the process. Here much depends on what your theology is of the continuing gifts of the Holy Spirit, as some say that they have received prophetic words from God as to when revival might hit a country or town.

But here we have to be careful. When I wrote the original edition of this book over eight years ago, many in Britain felt that the kind of misplaced outpouring of grief about Princess Diana's death indicated a spiritual longing that would be the precursor to revival. Not only did the intensity of feeling dissipate in the years after her death, but also the revival that so many British Christians understandably longed for has not happened. However, in other parts of the world vast numbers of people *have* been converted, and churches in some areas of the globe are growing exponentially. So maybe God *is* answering prayers but in places that we in the West do not expect.

In other words, I do not think that we have any right to dictate to God where He will work—that is His choice. If revival did come to Britain or the USA, that would be wonderful. But let us also rejoice that so much of the world today is seeing the gospel spread for the first time and that while revival is not being seen in London or Chicago, the work of God is being furthered today like never before in history.

Wesleyan Hymns

Some say the Methodist Revival was "born in song." It is a pity that although many songwriters today are excellent, we tend, certainly in Britain, mainly to sing modern compositions at the expense of the truly great hymns of the past. I am an alumnus of Westminster School, which Charles Wesley attended before going to Oxford; so I was privileged to sing his hymns at school as well as at church.

Consider my favorite Charles Wesley hymn, and contemplate the wonderful theological truths contained within it.

> And can it be that I should gain
> An interest in the Saviour's blood?
> Died He for me, who caused His pain?
> For me, who Him to death pursued?
> Amazing love! How can it be,
> That Thou, my God, shouldst die for me?
> Amazing love! How can it be,
> That Thou, my God, shouldst die for me?
>
> 'Tis mystery all: th' Immortal dies:
> Who can explore His strange design?
> In vain the firstborn seraph tries
> To sound the depths of love divine.
> 'Tis mercy all! Let earth adore,
> Let angel minds inquire no more.
> 'Tis mercy all! Let earth adore,
> Let angel minds inquire no more.
>
> He left His Father's throne above,
> So free, so infinite His grace—
> Emptied Himself of all but love,
> And bled for Adam's helpless race:

'Tis mercy all! Immense and free,
For O my God, it found out me!
'Tis mercy all! Immense and free,
For O my God, it found out me!

Long my imprisoned spirit lay
Fast bound in sin and nature's night;
Thine eye diffused a quickening ray—
I woke, the dungeon flamed with light;
My chains fell off, my heart was free,
I rose, went forth, and followed Thee.
My chains fell off, my heart was free,
I rose, went forth, and followed Thee.

No condemnation now I dread;
Jesus, and all in Him, is mine;
Alive in Him, my living Head,
And clothed in righteousness divine,
Bold I approach th' eternal throne,
And claim the crown, through Christ my own.
Bold I approach th' eternal throne,
And claim the crown, through Christ my own.

Evangelicals, Evangelists, and Fundamentalists

To many historians, the British equivalent in the wider sense of the Great Awakening is the Evangelical Revival, as that enables us to look at the non-Methodists who experienced a remarkable work of God as well as the Wesleys and Whitefield.

The term *evangelical* is often widely misunderstood. In Britain it is hopelessly confused in the secular media with the word *evangelist*, someone who spreads the gospel, as opposed to *evangelical*, someone who believes in it. In the USA it is frequently conflated with *fundamentalist*, and since Fundamentalism, so far as journalists and scholars are concerned, is now usually employed in sentences such as "Islamic fundamentalist Osama bin Laden is the mastermind behind the attacks on 9/11," we can be sure that it is not employed benignly.

Evangelical and *evangelist* both come from the Greek word translated *evangel* (ευανγελ), which as we have seen is the good news of salvation in and through Jesus Christ and His work on the cross. *Evangelical*, therefore, is a theological statement of what a Bible-oriented, Christ-centered Christian believes. Some writers have secularized the word to mean an enthusiast—"he is positively evangelical about the new make of car" or "she has become an evangelist for the teaching methods they use at the local school."

Fundamentalist is, strictly speaking, an American term, coined early in the twentieth century for Christians who supported a series of booklets about issues the authors and their sponsors regarded as the "fundamentals" of Christian truth. Properly understood this is all it means and should imply.

This is also why secular sociologists of religion, such as Professor Mark Juergensmeyer of the University of California, correctly, in my view, reject the use of the term for anything other than its foundational meaning. He refuses in his books on extremists in religion—Muslim, Hindu, Buddhist, Shinto—to use the term *fundamentalist* to describe any of these movements, arguing that to do so would be historically inappropriate. However, The Fundamentalism Project of the University of Chicago, led by Martin Marty, does use the word *fundamentalist* to cover a vast variety of religious beliefs and in my view does so incorrectly and certainly not with historical accuracy.

This is because *evangelical* is an eighteenth-century term, long pre-dating the word *fundamentalist*. This is also important because many of the features of Fundamentalism are not in fact theological but are culturally specific to the USA and therefore are doubly inaccurate when applied to theologically conservative Christians living in the wider world. Since now the vast majority of self-described evangelicals live outside the USA, in the Two-Thirds World, *evangelical* is therefore surely a better term to use.

EIGHT

The Dawn of Global Mission and Social Responsibility

T he terms *mission* and *social responsibility* do not often these days go hand in hand. In the nineteenth century evangelicals of all kinds ensured that they did, combining global missionary outreach with active social involvement that led to the abolition of child factory labor in Britain and slavery in both the British Empire and, alas through civil war, in the USA.

Inevitably as we get to more recent history I have to be more selective. It is possible that some of your favorite parts of Christian history have been left out. I have tried to omit any denominational biases and to avoid political partisanship. Let us see how history unfolds.

Bible and Flag?

As we saw at the end of the last chapter, as a result of the Great Awakening in the USA and the Evangelical Revival in Britain, Protestant missionaries were soon spreading the gospel across the globe.

175

In this they were also helped by the way in which the Catholic missions had run out of steam and in some cases even been abolished. The advantage of a free church is that it has no political constraints. This was not true with the Catholics. Due to many internal political upheavals—so brilliantly portrayed in the award-winning movie *The Mission*—the Pope abolished the Jesuit Order in 1773. The missionary inheritance of men such as Xavier and Ricci vanished, and although the Jesuits were eventually reestablished, other missionary societies were able to enter the gap they had left.

Missionaries these days are unfashionable in politically correct circles. They are linked to imperialism and to white Western colonialism. It is important therefore to remember in what follows that much of the missionary activity that took place was *before* the West conquered much of Asia and Africa. The "scramble for Africa" in which most of that continent was carved up between a few greedy European powers was in the 1880s, long after missionaries had been actively at work there.

Not only that, but an enormous proportion of Western missionaries were from the United States, which apart from a few conquests from Spain in the 1890s had virtually no overseas colonies at all. Not only that, but is bringing Western medicine and literacy so wrong? Was it wrong to abolish the odious slave trade? Colonialism is not something I think that we should defend, but although some missionaries sadly muddled Bible and flag and shared the racist attitudes of their fellow white colonizers, countless others did not and went for gospel reasons, not those of power and conquest.

Finally, in some parts of the world—notably in areas of the British Raj in India—the colonial authorities actually hindered missionary activity if they thought it would worsen relations with powerful local chiefs, such as the Maharajahs of the Indian subcontinent. So while things were certainly not always as they should have been, they were, I would argue, not nearly as bad as has been made out by critics, who in any case have a strong bias against Christianity itself and are not therefore the dispassionate witnesses they claim to be.

Let us look at three snapshots of great missionaries of the nineteenth century, out of the thousands from whom I could choose.

William Carey and India

William Carey (1761–1834) was one of the founders of the Baptist Missionary Society in 1792 and remains a deserved hero in Baptist circles to this day.

Carey is interesting in many ways. First, he was from a working-class family, not the usual upper-middle-class, university-educated missionary more normal at that time. He showed that you did not need to have a financially privileged background to work for God overseas.

Second, he proves that Bible and flag do not always go together. India until 1858 was ruled by the Honourable East India Company, a private (albeit government-approved) body, and the directors of the Company did not like Carey's missionary activities in the slightest, as they stirred up local Muslim and Hindu feeling. It took until 1829 and enormous pressure from evangelicals at home in Britain for British and also Danish missionaries to have freedom to evangelize in territory under Company rule.

Carey's famous phrase was, "Expect great things from God; attempt great things for God." His own life matched up to his statement, as did many of the pioneers of that time. It is important to remember that hygiene and medicine back then was often primitive in the extreme and that for countless brave Christians, going abroad to the mission field was a death sentence, as many left and did not return.

Hudson Taylor and China: The Open Century

It is with good cause that the nineteenth century is called "China's Open Century" in that it is the one time that missionaries from overseas were freely allowed into the country to preach the gospel. It is also perhaps the story of one of the most fruitful of all Western missions since there are now tens of millions of Chinese Christians, even though the Europeans were expelled in the 1950s. Today something like a quarter of the world's entire population are citizens of the People's Republic of China, and economic pundits sometimes predict that the twenty-first century might end up the "Chinese Century" in the same way that the twentieth was unquestionably the "American." Whether or not that will prove true, it is certain that while God's people in China continue to be oppressed, they demonstrate that no power on earth can prevent the mighty works of God.

China is also interesting in that apart from a few treaty ports such as Hong Kong and Macau (both once again Chinese), the West weakened China but never conquered it, and Western missionaries—thousands of Americans included—went far into the interior, well beyond the boundaries of the European and U.S. trade regions.

Until the late eighteenth century China was in effect closed to the West. Slowly but surely, though, Western diplomats and traders managed to break down the barriers, from the 1790s onward, with Canton (now Guangzhou) being the principal port of entry.

Much Western influence, it must be admitted, was profoundly wicked. The opium trade, sponsored by Britain, especially by the East India Company, was entirely evil and completely based upon Western greed regardless of the circumstances of the millions of poor Chinese addicts it ensnared. While much anti-Western political correctness is nonsense, there are large areas in which the West is genuinely guilty, and the narcotics trade is one of them.

Thankfully there were others in the West who wanted to bring *salvation* to the Chinese, not drugs. James Hudson Taylor (1832–1905) is the most famous of them. He founded the China Inland Mission, a society that under the name of Overseas Missionary Fellowship still exists and thrives today, now all over Asia.

Taylor was well aware of the cultural insensitivity of other Western missionaries. He was careful to have his own organization be controlled from the field, and not from back home in Britain where well-intentioned people might be ignorant of local circumstances. In fact,

CIM missionaries often wore local Chinese dress, to be able to better identify with the people among whom they worked.

As with Western missions to Africa and elsewhere, the CIM had a holistic approach, caring for the physical needs of the local people as well as the spiritual. There were CIM hospitals, schools, and similar institutions, and by 1949 the Chinese Christian student body was by far one of the biggest memberships of the International Fellowship of Evangelical Students.

Inevitably some in missionary areas were nicknamed "rice Christians"—those who professed some kind of conversion just to get better treatment or to look Western and sophisticated. Nominal Christianity is by no means restricted to the West, alas. But as we shall see, what makes China so fascinating is that there are now *millions* more Chinese Christians, over fifty years after the Communist takeover, than there were then. Rice Christians are not a thing of the past, but thank God, there are more genuine Christians there than ever before.

David Livingstone and Africa: Christians and the End of Slavery

The third great missionary I have chosen had few actual converts but changed an entire continent forever. This was David Livingstone (1813–1873).

When we think of the word *missionary*, those of us of a certain age and above often recall mental images of people in pith helmets in the midst of the African jungle. My own church as a child mainly had missionaries in Latin America and southeast Asia, but Africa is what came to mind for most of my contemporaries.

Africa was long a proud continent with a great, highly advanced civilization, something that in the twenty-first century we all too easily forget. Sadly, by the nineteenth century it was a part of the world in decline and disunity and thus all too prey to predatory European nations seeking glory and conquest. By 1900 most of Africa was under

European tutelage and was to remain so until the 1960s and 1970s (and longer in South Africa).

But when the missionaries came, large numbers of them were not pith-helmeted Europeans in league with the colonial powers but Americans—the Mary Knoll Fathers, for instance, and the Africa Inland Mission, an evangelical society formed in 1895.

Slavery was endemic to the continent until the British began to take action to end the pernicious trade—as seen, for example, by the closing scenes of the movie *Amistad*. We will soon discover that British evangelicals were at the heart of the movement to end slavery and that by and large they were able to do so peacefully, especially in those parts of West Africa that were coming under British control.

In Islamic East Africa it was otherwise. Slavery continued there much longer, as did the slave trade. It is ironic that many African-Americans have converted to Islam since it was in Muslim Africa that slavery as an institution lasted longer than anywhere else in the world. Just because the person who owns you is the same color as you does not make this evil any more acceptable than it was in the Old South.

One of those who knew this best was David Livingstone, the Scottish explorer and missionary and one of the few missionaries whose name is as known in the wider world as it is in the Christian.

When I was younger I used to read of Livingstone "discovering" parts of Africa. This is historically nonsense since the places he discovered had been familiar to the local inhabitants for centuries! Here I do agree with the politically correct—it is much better to say that he was the first *white* man to discover large areas of that continent.

But as far as he was concerned, he was there to do far more than to explore. He was officially attached to the London Missionary Society. His main task, as he saw it, was to rid "the open sore of Africa," the continued trade in slaves by the Muslim rulers of much of eastern Africa. In drawing the attention of the world to these terrible evils—the Royal Geographical Society in London possesses the shackles of slaves he helped free—he was able to play a major role in the eventual suppression of the trade.

Evangelicals are still involved in fighting slavery in Africa, which exists even now in some Muslim parts of the continent. Baroness Cox in Britain and many evangelical human rights organizations in the USA fight against continued slavery, with much being achieved by the U.S. Congress passing legislation and granting its support. Normally secular writers such as Nicholas Kristof of the *New York Times* praise the efforts of evangelicals abroad as much as they decry them at home. Livingstone's cause continues.

Christians and Social Concern

One tragedy of recent times is that evangelicals tend to be wary of social action, arguing that often such activity is a liberal substitute for preaching salvation. Sinners need to be saved, not just given soup!

Evangelicals of the nineteenth century would have been deeply puzzled by this dichotomy since, correctly I would argue, they held that such a division was entirely false and unbiblical. As one of the greatest of them, Lord Shaftesbury, once put it, "The God who made men's souls made their bodies also." In other words, it is a question of both/and, not either/or, a point made in the twentieth century by American evangelicals such as Francis Schaeffer who also did not see any contradiction between evangelism and social concern.

The evangelicals at whom we shall look embodied the approach that the parable of the Samaritan still applies today—to love your neighbor as yourself implies your neighbor's physical needs as well as spiritual.

I get the impression that for some in the USA the question is in fact whether or not the *state* should do these things. They have no problem with faith-based groups working in the inner city or establishing hospitals, but they feel that the state as such should play no part. That is a different argument altogether and to me, as a British outsider, is more allied to U.S. partisan politics, which I wish to avoid. I will therefore leave that discussion to others!

Once again we can look at history through the lives of particularly outstanding individuals, each one of whom played a major role and significantly, I think, two of them by being involved in politics. Here I am deliberately taking one from the political right, William Wilberforce, and the other, an eminent Whig, Lord Shaftesbury, from the liberal left. We will then go on to look at how evangelicals were similarly involved in the USA in the abolitionist movement. Although it took a war to obtain freedom for the slaves, the moral climate that made decent Americans realize that slavery was no longer acceptable owes an enormous debt to faithful Christians and not to guns.

William Wilberforce and the Abolition of Slavery

By the eighteenth century the consensus in Britain was that slavery was an evil that should no longer continue. There were not many domestic slaves in England, but the ports of Liverpool and Bristol had played a major role as points in the triangle between West Africa and the American colonies—the Caribbean part of which, we should remember, stayed British, such as Trinidad and Jamaica. There is now a museum to the evils of the trade in Bristol. Not a few aristocratic fortunes were founded on the proceeds of slavery and the sugar trade. But by the 1790s many civilized people in Britain knew that the whole business was barbaric and should be ended. These included a large group of evangelicals living in what is now a southern suburb of London called Clapham. Mainly known for their godly lifestyle and concerns, others nicknamed them the Clapham Sect, as they are still known today.

They realized that although, for example, the Royal Navy could achieve much in ending the pernicious traffic, ultimately it would need an act of political will for Britain formally to abolish both slavery and the slave trade. Fortunately, or one might say providentially, there was such a politician among them. This was William Wilberforce (1759–1833), a Tory Member of Parliament (the House of Commons) from 1784–1825, a prosperous businessman, and a good friend of the Prime Minister for most of this period, William Pitt.

Wilberforce, with his connections and ability, could easily have held high office. But instead he devoted his life as an active and open evangelical in days when such beliefs were not fashionable to the cause of freeing the slaves. The final liberation took place just after his death, although he knew it was coming, and he is a wonderful example of what the dogged persistence of one godly man can achieve, even though it takes a lifetime to accomplish it.

In 1807 he succeeded in getting slavery abolished in Britain, in 1813 he was able to get missionaries allowed into parts of the British Empire from which they had been excluded, and in 1834, just after his death, slavery was abolished throughout the British Empire.

Lord Shaftesbury and the Abolition of Child Labor

Anthony Ashley-Cooper (1801–1885), Earl of Shaftesbury, is commemorated in a famous London street, Shaftesbury Avenue. He was a wealthy landowner and hereditary member of the House of Lords. His family history is interesting. One of his ancestors was one of Britain's most eminent eighteenth-century Deists, and his twenty-first-century descendant as Earl was murdered in tragic circumstances a few years ago. We are saved not by our family roots but by our own individual relationship with Jesus Christ as our personal Savior and Lord, and the Cooper family is a prime example.

Shaftesbury was a Whig politician and was able to persuade the rather godless Whig Prime Minister, Lord Palmerston, to appoint many evangelicals to key posts in the Church of England. Whatever Palmerston's morals, he always listened to Shaftesbury's advice.

Shaftesbury, like Wilberforce, gave up political advancement for himself to aid the cause of others, in this instance that of young children from poor homes forced to work in dangerous jobs in factories and up chimneys as sweeps. Countless children died in easily avoidable accidents until Shaftesbury was able to persuade Parliament to pass appropriate legislation to ban such barbaric working habits. The Ten Hours Act of 1847 and the Factory Act of 1874 were two of the key Acts that prevented the abuse of child labor.

Shaftesbury was involved in many of the leading evangelical bodies of his day—the Church Missionary Society, the YMCA, and the Evangelical Alliance. The Shaftesbury Society still exists to perpetuate his work.

American Evangelicals and the Fight Against Slavery

Slavery in the USA is an unavoidable issue, even in the twenty-first century, as in many parts of North America the hideous psychological damage that slavery inflicted upon owners and slaves alike still mars relations between those of European and African ancestry respectively. As one of my former pupils in Virginia once put it, Sunday is still often the most segregated day of the week, and while many evangelical churches are doing their best to overcome that—Grace Community Church in California, where John MacArthur preaches, is a notable example of Sunday integration succeeding—there are plenty of other instances where on God's day white Christians go to one church while their black fellow Christians attend another. Some of this has to do with preference in matters such as worship style, but in all too many other cases it is the legacy of the terrible events of the seventeenth to nineteenth centuries, when one human being could literally own another.

One of the tragedies of the ante-bellum period (as the pre-Civil War era is called in the USA) is that there were evangelicals on both sides of the divide, a split that should never have happened. Denominations separated over the slavery issue—the existence of *Southern* Baptists is one example—and friends went their different ways. President Lincoln—no evangelical himself—noted with dismay when the Civil War began in 1861 that Americans on both sides of it were praying to the same God and reading the same Bible. To be fair, while most northerners ended up wanting to see the end of slavery, historians reckon that they also usually presumed that it would not be abolished in the southern slave-owning states. A northern invasion to end slavery was never in the cards, and it was the southern declaration of independence in 1861 that sparked four years of unbelievably brutal civil war and carnage and Lincoln's decision in 1862—after the war had already begun—to abolish slavery and emancipate the slaves. Emancipation was thus a result of the war and not its original cause.

Not only that, many southern generals in the war, such as the great Robert E. Lee, owned no slaves themselves and fought for the South on patriotic grounds rather than to defend an evil institution. Another famous general, "Stonewall" Jackson, used to teach the Bible to African-Americans in his hometown even though to do so was technically illegal. This is not in any way to defend those who took up the southern cause, but it is something that we should not forget.

Many writers whom we otherwise revere, such as the great Bible commentator Virginius Dabney, whose theological works are still read with much profit, were supporters of slavery, something we overlook today. Likewise, while the evangelical abolitionist John Brown is regarded as a hero, the notion of taking up arms in a Christian cause, however noble, and his resort to violence is something that should make us all uneasy.

Some of the major anti-slavery activists, such as Harriet Beecher Stowe (1811–1896), author of the wonderful story *Uncle Tom's Cabin*, which was published in 1852, are justly famous for drawing a whole nation's attention to the evils of slavery and, in her case, in a way that anyone could understand.

Often forgotten, though, is one of the writers and activists who inspired Stowe so much, the fascinating Theodore Dwight Weld (1803–1895). He was a convert of the major nineteenth-century American evangelist Charles Finney, and he dedicated much of his earlier life to advocating the abolition of slavery within churches in the USA. His book *Slavery As It Is: The Testimony of a Thousand Witnesses* came out in 1839 and sold over one hundred thousand copies in its first year.

He married a southern, anti-slavery activist, Angelina Grimké, who along with her sister Sarah had been forced to flee their South Carolina home because of their abolitionist stand. Weld's other book, *Slavery in the West Indies*, was designed to show how slavery could be successfully abolished. Sadly, his pleas fell on deaf ears. In fact, the conditions of slaves got worse in following years right up to the Civil War since slave owners became all the more terrified after abortive slave revolts convinced them that they needed to be harsher than ever in order to keep their servile population in check.

Along with two wealthy businessmen brothers, Arthur and Lewis Tappan, Weld also organized the American Anti-Slavery Society, founded by them in 1833. Weld was, like Charles Finney, also involved in Oberlin College in Ohio, which was the first American college not merely to admit men and women together but students of African ancestry as well. Weld also took his campaign to Washington, D.C., where he supported the efforts of former President John Quincy Adams to force Congress to accept the petitions of American citizens outraged by slavery—southerners had done all possible to prevent such petitions from being heard. Here the campaign took a while—Weld visited D.C. in 1837, but not until 1844 did Adams succeed.

Some Other Movements in Britain

Back in Britain, besides evangelical social action there was considerable effort, especially as literacy improved (something evangelicals fostered), to help people read God's Word for themselves.

The Religious Tract Society was formed in 1799—an ancestor of groups today like Good News Publishers that aim to put the Christian message in succinct forms in tracts. The British and Foreign Bible Society, linked with spreading the Bible worldwide, was formed in 1804.

Also crucial were the Sunday school movements, which helped children from deprived homes discover the truth of the Christian message and helped encourage literacy as well. Methodist Sunday schools began as early as 1769, and evangelical Anglicans founded the Church of England Sunday School Society in 1786.

The Rise of Liberalism: Darwin and Huxley

Alas, the nineteenth century did not just see evangelical activity but also the origin of theories that were to inflict such devastating harm in the twentieth. Perhaps the greatest of these was Darwinism.

Here I should add that many evangelicals in Britain and the USA espouse a moderate form of Darwinism, one that they believe is fully compatible with Scripture and complements the biblical accounts rather than attacking them. While I fully accept them as genuinely born-again evangelical Christians—which is certainly the case of all those whom I have the pleasure of knowing—I for one, although I am a historian and not a scientist, sympathize far more on *theological* grounds with friends of mine working at places such as the Discovery Institute in Seattle. They, however, are what is called old earth creationists, and they in turn are criticized by other evangelicals—such as the well-known preacher John MacArthur who prefers to stick to a six-thousand-year timetable and a young earth interpretation. So evangelicals divide among themselves on this issue and within what one might broadly call Creationism as well.

This is not the place to enter the science vs. Christianity debate, and I imagine that readers of this book have their own theological opinions on this discussion. Evangelical theistic evolutionists are also right to warn that we must be careful not to adopt a God of the gaps approach, and it is sadly true that while new discoveries regularly seem to bolster the case for God's creating the universe, nonetheless atheists always seem to be able to find escape clauses that enable them to continue in unbelief.

But if one looks at the *historical* results of what is called Social Darwinism, upon which I am qualified as a historian to write, I would argue that the effects are very disturbing in terms of the rise of racist attitudes, Western imperialism, and Nazi practices, let alone a materialistic worldview.

Charles Darwin (1809–1882) and his book *The Origin of Species* created a revolution in thinking that has not ceased for these past 150 years. Evolution as a general idea was not entirely new, but Darwin gave it scientific credence through his discoveries and thereby, in the eyes of most people in the West, discredited what the Bible teaches about the origins of life and of humanity in particular.

Darwin was not by nature a public speaker. So his most ardent disciple, Thomas Huxley, took up the task with enthusiasm. He preached Darwinism up and down the land, and significantly he used it to attack religion, something that humanist/secular scientists have not hesitated to do ever since, down to Richard Dawkins in our own day.

Today members of the Darwin, Huxley, and (John Maynard) Keynes families have intermarried, with descendants not far from where I am writing this. Huxley's descendants include the novelist Aldous Huxley and the eminent scientist Sir Julian Huxley—scientists produce dynasties as much as politicians!

In the twenty-first century numerous scientists are also keen evangelical Christians. And in many secular universities the number of scientists in campus Christian groups often by far exceeds those in the humanities, the latter area having been infiltrated far more by postmodernism. It is now much harder to argue that science and faith are incompatible than it was when Huxley first attacked those who defended the Christian position. Scientific discoveries have also helped render the case for non-theistic Darwinism far more unlikely, and in the past few years major finds in mitochondrial DNA (the DNA you inherit from your mother) have suggested that everyone alive today contains the DNA of just one woman who lived just a few hundred thousand years ago (as shown by such men as Oxford University professor Brian Sykes and London's Natural History Museum's Christopher

Stringer). Similarly, the discovery not only of the Big Bang but also of the extreme unlikelihood of life itself—the conditions in the early universe having to be so amazingly finely tuned for life to appear at all—suggest that much of what the secular Darwinists used to hurl at Christians is now impossible for *them* to defend.

It is, of course, the work of the Holy Spirit in conviction of sin that brings about conversion. Nonetheless, looking at things from the perspective of the twenty-first century rather than that of the mid-nineteenth, it does seem that the task of apologetics is now just as necessary as ever but is built, as far as science is concerned, on increasingly stronger evidence.

The social effects of Darwinism were dire. Coming as they did from the Anglo-Saxon part of the West, they reinforced the feelings of racial superiority of white Anglo-Saxons in Britain, Germany, and the USA, not only in relation to those of African or Asian ancestry, but also to what they regarded as inferior white races and, above all, toward Jews. This was the major period of Western colonialism, and the same time saw anti-Semitism rise as never before. The wealthy classes used this as a means to justify looking down upon their supposed social inferiors. The doctrines that led to Nazism and the Holocaust also arose in this era, and Darwinism was inevitably used to bolster the claims of those who both professed and practiced such odious beliefs.

NINE

The Great Century:
Christianity Becomes Global

Christianity in the twenty-first century is a truly global faith. Vast swaths of territory that were once pagan and where the name of Jesus was unknown are now filled with dynamic and growing Christian churches.

This is principally as a result of growth in the twentieth century. It was in the nineteenth century that missionaries poured out from the West to as many parts of the globe as they could find, in order to fulfill the command of Jesus' Great Commission. But it was the last century, the twentieth, that bore the fruit.

We have touched upon that exciting story already, but we will now look at it in more depth.

The Century of War, Ideology, and Violence

In many ways the Christian growth of the twentieth century was a paradox since so much of it went horribly wrong, not just in the

West but everywhere else as well. Never has there been such carnage and depravity as in the hundred years gone by. False gods of modern variety have come and gone, leaving death, mayhem, and massacre in their respective wakes.

Yet it could be, I would argue, precisely because of all this that the church has grown and been so blessed. For if ever there was a century in which man's own inventions—colonialism, racism, Fascism, Communism, consumerism—have been tried, it was then; and if ever there was also a time period in which such man-made dreams have been proved false, it has been the same century.

Even Communism, which looked so powerful and invincible, disintegrated like a pack of cards in the years 1989–1991. China theoretically remains Communist but, many political experts would argue, in name only, as a system of control. Capitalism is now thriving there as much as human rights are being suppressed. The failure of Mao to deliver a Marxist paradise on earth during the carnage of the Cultural Revolution—in which millions of innocent people died—probably did more than anything else to convince many millions of Chinese of the eternal truth of salvation in Jesus Christ.

So let us remember all this as we survey twentieth-century history. It was possibly the worst ever in history in terms of death and horror, with atrocities committed on a scale hitherto unimaginable. Yet it is also the time when more people became Christians than at any other.

Christianity is now at its strongest in the parts of the world in which most people live. We must also fleetingly consider Europe, where the faith is now in decline because some of the most prominent liberal theologians of the twentieth century were either Europeans or originated there.

Humanistic optimism at the end of the nineteenth century had been boundless—what could mankind (especially white Anglo-Saxons) not achieve? Those of European ancestry ruled over most of the globe, Darwin—or more correctly, the proselytism of his disciple Huxley—had rendered God redundant, and discovery and invention were speeding up the pace of progress as never before.

Then came World War I—the Great War as it was then called. In the muddy fields of Flanders, not only did millions of young men die—many of them the intellectual cream of their generation—but so too did the ludicrous optimism of the theological liberals and that of the late Victorian era. The far more realistic biblical view of humanity—that we are all fallen sinners—should have been vindicated upon many a university campus or middle-class household. The liberal view of the goodness of man was shown to be entirely false (and would be again, with a vengeance, in 1939–1945).

From Neo-Orthodoxy to Demythologizing

Yet what we had instead was a fuzzy, halfway house theology that recognized the failings of Liberalism and yet was unable to make a full return to biblically orthodox theology. This was called Neo-Orthodoxy, and in non-evangelical circles it retains its power on many university campuses to this day.

The most famous Neo-Orthodox theologian was Karl Barth (1886–1968), a Swiss pastor and thinker whose influence is as strong in such circles now as during his lifetime. He understood that Liberalism was untenable but was profoundly affected by nineteenth-century thinkers such as the Danish philosopher Søren Kierkegaard, who asked questions about the nature of existence and related topics. Barth is hard to summarize, but I think he can best be described as teaching that God is completely "other" or innately different from humanity and that He can only really be understood, according to Barth, from His words to us rather than through human reason. This did at least mean that Barth took the Bible seriously, and it is interesting that his favorite book was Romans, the same epistle that had so influenced Luther centuries before.

One of Liberalism's greatest myths is that modern man does not like the supernatural, and it is therefore necessary to take that element out of the Christian faith in order to make it acceptable to contemporary audiences. I describe this as a myth because simple observation shows that it is simply untrue! Secularists remain as uninterested in Christianity as ever, even with the liberal supernatural-free version. Meanwhile, for example, on many a university campus, from Charlottesville, Virginia to Cambridge, England, gospel-faithful, evangelical churches are bursting at the seams, with many students and faculty becoming Christians, significantly perhaps more among scientists than those in the humanities. Globally supernatural Christianity is thriving as never before, with millions becoming Christians in countries where, in 1900, hardly anyone had even heard of the Christian faith, let alone become a Christian.

Nevertheless, the idea of removing supernatural accretions from Christianity, as liberals would see it, or "demythologizing" the faith, to use their term, became and remains an article of profound belief among liberals in the old mainstream denominations. By the 1950s Karl Barth was less influential in such circles, and Rudolph Bultmann (1884–1976) rose in eminence. His aim was to demythologize Christianity or, as he put it, to make it "clearer to modern man."

As evangelicals we do have to admit that such people were well-meaning and sincere and at the same time clearly see that they were entirely mistaken. The problems in such an approach very rapidly became apparent. If you remove the supernatural core of the Christian faith, how do you decide what stays in? Who is entitled to say what remains and why? Everything becomes an entirely subjective judgment, with one theologian allowing some things while others reject them, all on entirely personal rather than objective grounds and criteria.

Ultimately either one does believe in the supernatural or one does not. Mushy halfway thinking has ended up convincing nobody, let alone secular western Europe, from which such people came. As the early-twentieth-century Catholic thinker G. K. Chesterton (now best known for his Father Brown detective series) once put it, once people stop believing in God, they do not believe in nothing but rather in anything. Most of western Europe is now materialistic and secular, and those people who do have religious beliefs turn not to liberal

Christianity but to fuzzy New Age thinking, or, in the case of growing numbers of white Europeans, to Islam. Liberals still exist in the old denominations, but those professing Christianity are now increasingly evangelicals, including large numbers of believers of African origin now settled in the West. Liberals might control the official hierarchies, but it is more and more evangelicals who dominate the actual churches and who sit in the pews.

C. S. Lewis (1898–1963), a devout High Church Christian, saw this very clearly and wrote in 1952 in his famous book *Mere Christianity*:

> "I'm ready to accept Jesus Christ as a moral teacher, but I don't accept his claim to be God." That is the one thing we must not say. A man who was merely a man and said the sort of things Jesus said would not be a great moral teacher. He would either be a lunatic—on a level with a man who says he is a poached egg—or else he would be the Devil of Hell. . . . Either this man was, and is, the Son of God, or else a madman or something worse.

No evangelical could put it better, and we would surely all agree with what Lewis says. Christianity has God's redemption at its core, not some lowest-common-denominator, warm, fuzzy teaching about being nice to everyone, which you do not have to be a religious person to accept. It is, I would say, no coincidence that in the twenty-first century it is the liberal churches that are dying and the evangelical ones that are growing, as ordinary people are not even remotely deceived by what liberals proclaim.

Evangelicals and Fundamentalists

One of the many mistakes that the secular media make is in conflating two quite separate groups—*evangelicals* and *fundamentalists*. This, I would argue, is a historical mistake since from the 1940s onward the two groupings have been quite separate, as some secular writers are now slowly coming to understand.

Fundamentalists, as we saw, are those who followed the teachings published in booklet form in the early twentieth century on the *fundamentals* of the Christian faith, especially around 1910–1915. Most evangelicals would sign up to the majority of these very easily since in the main they were simply a defense of the key doctrines of Scripture. Others, such as Dispensationalism/Premillennialism, were controversial to many.

However, I think it fair to say that the main difference between Fundamentalism and what we would now call historic Evangelicalism is as much cultural as anything else and is particularly an American phenomenon.

Theologically conservative American Christians felt understandably under siege as the twentieth century progressed because of the takeover of so many historic denominations by liberals who now hardly believed any of the Bible, let alone its core truths, and also because of the rapid increase in secularism, embodied by the triumph of godless Darwinism among ordinary people as well as among intellectuals. The world seemed against them, and they retreated into a tight-knit world of their own. This mentality was wholly reactive and also permanently on the defensive.

Scripturally, however, living in a cozy rabbit hole was not a viable option. In addition, Fundamentalism was also profoundly anti-intellectual, neglecting to see from the Bible that our minds are part of being created in the image of God.

By the 1940s growing numbers of fundamentalists, notably the American thinker and writer Carl F. H. Henry (1913–2003), realized that this defensive, escapist way of thinking was simply not scriptural. This new group came to be called *evangelicals*, a much older term going back to the Evangelical Awakening of the eighteenth century and to giants such as Jonathan Edwards and George Whitefield and to England in the nineteenth century, especially William Wilberforce and Lord Shaftesbury.

Withdrawal, Henry showed in his 1947 book *The Uneasy Conscience of Modern Fundamentalism*, was not a biblical option. Nor was anti-intellectualism. As he, Francis Schaeffer (1912–1984), and in Britain Martyn Lloyd-Jones (1899–1981), J. I. Packer (b. 1926), and John Stott (b. 1921) all demonstrated, Christianity was *true* and therefore entirely intellectually defensible and justifiable.

The years since then have seen a major renaissance in thoughtful, biblically involved, evangelical Christianity. We will later briefly examine the careers of Schaeffer, Billy Graham, and Lloyd-Jones, three of the key players.

Fundamentalists now also call themselves evangelicals, and in strict *theological* terms that would be fair since they believe in the same scriptural core truths as evangelicals. However, it is also, alas, true to say that they live in the same culturally isolated ghettos as before, while evangelicals have gone out to proclaim Christ as both Savior and Lord in the world around them, following the biblical mandate to be *in* the world but emphatically not *of* it.

Since the 1970s it has also been evident that Evangelicalism is a global phenomenon, something that became apparent at the Lausanne Convention in 1974, at which evangelicals from Billy Graham to Francis Schaeffer spoke, along with the representatives of millions of Christians from the developing world. While Fundamentalism is therefore an American phenomenon, Evangelicalism is worldwide and growing.

Vatican II

While I have mainly concentrated upon biblical Christianity in this chapter, we should not overlook developments in the Roman Catholic Church. We will later discuss Pope John Paul II, probably the best known Catholic of recent centuries.

Major theological shifts sometimes happen by accident, and this is certainly true of the theological revolution that hit the Catholic Church in the mid-twentieth century. In 1958 Pope Pius XII, an austere diplomat now best known for his controversial relations with the Nazi Third Reich, died, and the Cardinals elected the Patriarch of Venice, Angelo Roncalli, a seventy-six-year-old prelate they probably thought would be no more than a stop-gap appointment. But the new Pope, who gave himself the name John XXIII, proved to be a revolutionary, and not just because, unlike his recent predecessors, he was from a humble background.

He summoned, for the first time in decades, a major Council of the Church, which met from 1962–1965. Pope John XXIII died during it in 1963, being succeeded by Pope Paul VI, who shared his reforming zeal. Known as Vatican II, it soon transformed Catholic theology, aiming to take it into the modern age. With transportation so improved, prelates were able to come from literally all over the world to sit, discuss, and debate, all encouraged by the Pope.

Two of his Encyclicals expressed the new mood. The first was on the "social teaching" of the Church, a set of beliefs on the nature of society still followed by more radically inclined Catholics to this day. The second, *Pacem in Terris* ("Peace on Earth"), emphasized the equality of all races and also strongly condemned the growing arms race between the superpowers.

With the election of the theologically far more conservative Pope John Paul II in 1978 (and his equally conservative successor, the German Pope Benedict XVI in 2005), radical Catholics still look back to Vatican II as a golden age, especially liberal Catholics in places such as the USA and Britain. Catholics in many developing countries, like evangelicals, tend to be far more theologically conservative.

Ecumenically Vatican II also created a thaw with Protestant churches since both John XXIII and Paul VI were keen on ecumenical dialogue. This, however, tended to be with the so-called mainstream churches—Archbishop Michael Ramsey of Canterbury notably visited Rome, for instance—rather than with evangelicals.

Theologically, from a biblical point of view, nothing really changed since the key Catholic doctrines to which Protestants have objected since the Reformation did not change. Changes that did take place tended to be among grass-roots Catholics in majority Protestant countries such as Britain and the USA, marked by the emergence of Catholics who were deeply influenced by evangelical theology, such as a well-known group in Ann Arbor, Michigan—the Word of God Community—while retaining nominal membership in the Roman Catholic Church.

Azusa Street and After

Today, in the twenty-first century, an enormous percentage of evangelicals would also call themselves Pentecostal or if they are in ordinary denominations, charismatics.

As with the issue of Dispensationalism that we examined in an earlier chapter, writing on this issue is a theological minefield. The claim that the miraculous sign gifts of the early church—most notably that of speaking in tongues or using special heaven-sent languages—remains as deeply controversial as when the Pentecostal movement got going back at the turn of the twentieth century. Few things still divide evangelicals more, especially as some, notably in Australia, claim that it is in fact impossible to be both evangelical and charismatic/Pentecostal at the same time, while others, though not so inclined themselves, say that Pentecostalism is the evangelical future. So with that important caveat in mind, I will try as carefully as possible to examine the phenomenal growth of Pentecostalism and its allied charismatic movement.

While small numbers of Protestants, such as the eighteenth-century "French Prophets" who visited Britain, have been "speaking in tongues" for centuries, the Pentecostal movement as we now know it began in a church on Azusa Street in Los Angeles, California in 1906. The name *Pentecostal* arose from the Day of Pentecost recorded in the book of Acts, when the apostles spoke in "other tongues" (2:4) to their international, multinational audience.

Historically, the "other tongues" of Acts has been interpreted as different earthly languages that the speakers had not learned—everyone present at Pentecost could understand the apostles in their own languages. So I think it is more accurate biblically to say that the idea of tongues as a miraculous sign language from God should be understood as the unintelligible language to which Paul refers in his epistle to the Corinthians.

What makes Pentecostalism controversial is its theology that speaking in miraculous languages is a sign from God that a *baptism of the Holy Spirit*, a special anointing from God subsequent to conversion, has taken place. Incidents in the book of Acts are seen by Pentecostals and charismatics as normative, and baptism with the Holy Spirit is seen as leading to a deeper kind of Christian life and effectiveness, a teaching that, needless to say, causes controversy among evangelicals who do not hold such views or who have not shared in such experiences.

Within a short time Pentecostal denominations appeared, the best-known being the Assemblies of God, although there are now dozens of differing kinds and emphases worldwide. Pentecostals soon started to practice what they felt were other miraculous sign gifts such as healing, prophecy, words of knowledge, and in the case of some more recent charismatic groups in Britain and the USA a revived gift of being an apostle as well.

By the 1960s Pentecostal theology had also spread into mainstream denominations, known as the Charismatic or Renewal Movement. Now people in different Christian groups were speaking in tongues or practicing healing ministries.

A fascinating and more recent development is the mixing of Reformed theology with charismatic belief, something that is perhaps more prevalent in Britain, where one large charismatic denomination, New Frontiers, has a strongly Reformed leadership, as opposed to the USA where such a combination is still perhaps in its infancy. Many Reformed charismatics would claim deeply to be influenced by Martyn Lloyd-Jones, who while not a charismatic himself nevertheless believed in the continuation of the sign gifts but without such gifts being a necessary evidence of baptism with the Holy Spirit. While Calvin was firmly cessationist, this group strongly follows Reformed theology on all the major doctrines of grace. Because many in the Southern Baptist

Convention are legitimately being called Reformed because they too follow Scripture (and Calvin) on that issue, I think it legitimate to allow for those British and American charismatics who call themselves Reformed to be allowed to do so as well.

Needless to say, Lloyd-Jones's views on this subject, preached at Westminster Chapel in the 1960s in his series on the epistle to the Ephesians and on the first chapter of John's Gospel, were very controversial among his non-charismatic followers! They can be read in detail in the relevant volume of the Ephesians series of his works—where he refers to the "sealing of the Spirit"—and in his book *Joy Unspeakable*.

While not charismatic myself—like Lloyd-Jones I would separate belief in the continuation of the sign gifts from any automatic link with baptism or sealing in the Spirit—I would want to argue that many in the overall charismatic/Pentecostal movement today are primarily evangelicals who also believe in their particular theology on charismatic gifts. Obviously there are major theological problems (to say the least) from an evangelical standpoint with those in the Pentecostal movement who also preach a gospel of wealth, which I cannot see as remotely biblical. But many others would identify themselves very much as evangelicals first and foremost, and today in many countries they would seek very actively to come together with fellow evangelicals who, like Calvin in the past, would be cessationist over spiritual gifts.

What has worried evangelicals is that many in the various renewal movements emphasize experience over doctrine—namely, they believe that experience determines doctrine and not the other way around. This was a source of anxiety to Martyn Lloyd-Jones as well, as his book *Joy Unspeakable* makes clear. This anxiety has proved all too true in the past. But then we ought never to forget that all sorts of emotional outbursts and physical phenomena accompanied the work of Jonathan Edwards in the Great Awakening, and interestingly enough it was the discovery of that which has led not a few in charismatic circles to discover that Reformed doctrine might be all right after all!

On the validity and results of this issue, as the Chinese politician Zhou Enlai (who died in 1976) said when asked about the effects of the French Revolution, it is perhaps too early to tell. One can but hope that what has been a very divisive issue among evangelicals in the twentieth century will not be so in the twenty-first, especially if Pentecostals and charismatics decide to identify themselves primarily as Bible-based evangelicals, as some are now doing.

Pope John Paul II

In the original version of this book it was necessary, being produced by a secular publisher, to be more neutral than I am in this new edition. So I have removed the sections about people such as Dietrich Bonhoeffer and Mother Teresa since, while they are important in their own way, they did not make as great a difference to the growth of Bible-based Christianity in the twentieth century—and, in the case of Mother Teresa, she had universalist views that we as Christians would surely reject.

I am retaining Pope John Paul II (Karol Wojtyla; 1920–2005), not because of his theology, large parts of which we as evangelicals would also reject, but because of the enormous global impact he had during his Papacy, not least his pivotal role in helping to end Communist rule in eastern/central Europe, a development toward freedom and liberty for millions for which everyone, evangelicals and atheists alike, can be profoundly thankful.

After 1945 Stalin, the odious and bloodthirsty Soviet dictator, once joked, "How many divisions has the Pope?" We should not forget that Stalin was responsible for the deaths of tens of millions more innocent people than even Adolf Hitler.

During that period, when Soviet divisions occupied most of central and eastern Europe and created the Iron Curtain, it looked as if millions would be permanently under Communist dictatorship. The Soviet bloc seemed impregnable, and since no one wanted nuclear annihilation and World War III to get rid of it, it appeared to the West, including to so-called "realists" in American foreign policy such as Henry Kissinger, that there was nothing that we could do about it either.

Needless to say, Christians were repressed throughout the Soviet bloc, although local conditions did vary from time to time and from country to country. As someone who visited many evangelical students behind the Iron Curtain during this period—unofficially in my case—I can testify to the hardships with which they had to live all the time, with privations that we would find hard to bear in the West.

While some Christians accepted such a state of affairs as inevitable—the early church had lived with persecution for centuries, and Protestants in most of central Europe had suffered similarly from groups such as the Jesuits—others did not.

Among those not accepting Soviet hegemony was a Catholic priest from Krakow, the city in which Oscar Schindler had rescued thousands of Polish Jews during the Second World War (immortalized in the movie *Schindler's List*). This priest was Karol Wojtyla. His training was illegal, and he continued to suffer under Communism throughout his ministry, which saw him become first the Archbishop of Krakow, an ancient diocese, and then a Cardinal.

Polish Catholicism is strongly Marian, and Cardinal Wojtyla was no exception. The Polish Communists looked upon the Catholics with grave suspicion, and this was good news for evangelicals. Baptists were Protestants and therefore not Catholic, which made them acceptable to the anti-Catholic Polish government.

In 1978 the Italian Pope Paul VI died. His successor, as had been the case for centuries, was another Italian, the Venetian John Paul I. But this new Pope died unexpectedly after a reign of only a few weeks. This created a crisis in Rome, and the rival Italian candidates canceled each other out. The result was a complete surprise: the first non-Italian Pope for hundreds of years, Karol Wojtyla, who gave himself the papal title of John Paul II, in tribute to his predecessor.

Theologically he was a conservative, holding on to Catholic doctrines and emphases that evangelicals would reject. But his international impact was massive, and not just because he rapidly became the most traveled Pope in history.

The impact his election had on the suffering church under Communism was tremendous, not least because the head of the Catholic Church was one of them. He could be their voice and, being outside Soviet control, could speak freely to the world on their behalf. We now know the Soviets were ultimately behind the unsuccessful attempt to kill him early in his Papacy.

In Poland a Catholic-inspired free trade union, Solidarity, began in 1979 under the leadership of a devout Catholic shipyard worker, Lech Walesa, in Gdansk. Although this was crushed, the spark it lit proved impossible to extinguish. Also, the election of a comparatively moderate Soviet leader in 1985, Mikhail Gorbachev, put in office a Russian who realized that the Soviet bloc could not be effectively crushed forever.

So when in 1989 the repressed countries of central and southeast Europe erupted in protest, World War III did not begin. By the end of that epochal year Communism had been overthrown, with real bloodshed only in Romania. By 1991 even the once mighty and seemingly invincible Soviet Union itself collapsed, effectively imploding from within.

There were, of course, plenty of other reasons for the collapse of the Soviet bloc, not least the realization by many in the USA that the "evil empire," as it was called, was not inevitable and might end without nuclear annihilation. While this is certainly true, and while the causes were many, the role of John Paul II was nonetheless enormous. He showed that ideas are more important than armies and that faith really can move what many saw as immovable mountains.

So while we can look back on his spiritual impact as being mixed, as seen from an evangelical standpoint, the fact that millions of people now live in freedom and that hundreds of thousands of our fellow Christians are no longer persecuted is in God's providence very much due to Karol Wojtyla and his courageous, lifelong stand for freedom.

Francis Schaeffer

Francis Schaeffer (1912–1984) was the greatest evangelical apologist of the twentieth century.

Born in Pennsylvania of immigrant German ancestry, Schaeffer began his career as a Presbyterian minister in the USA. Although highly effective locally, he was not then exceptional, except perhaps in empathy and kindness, and no one would have predicted the great future he would later enjoy.

Initially he branched out into ministry for children. It was this that took him to Europe after the devastation caused there by the Second World War. He met with local evangelicals such as Martyn Lloyd-Jones in Britain and felt a powerful calling from God to shift his ministry away from the USA to the spiritually needy and economically wrecked countries of western Europe, which had not long been liberated from war and Nazism.

He began his ministry in Switzerland, and the story of a tiny beginning in a Swiss village has been wonderfully told by his widow, Edith, in her account of their home, L'Abri, the French word for "shelter." Her book is simply titled *L'Abri*. What is so fascinating is that none of this was planned ahead—God was leading providentially all the way, one step at a time, until the ministry that began as an acorn reaching out to local children became a worldwide outreach with thousands from all over the globe coming every year to hear the gospel faithfully proclaimed.

Francis Schaeffer has often, mistakenly I think, been called a philosopher. He certainly dealt with the empty, vacuous philosophies of the twentieth century and showed them to be false. But I think, as he once suggested to me, that he was primarily an evangelist—something at which he was deeply blessed by God over many decades on a one to one basis at L'Abri and then to millions through his books, which came out first in the 1960s and continued until his death in 1984.

He was also, I would argue, an apologist—his books such as *Escape from Reason* demonstrate this very clearly. While it is true that later on he made some historical mistakes, as we all do in considering large time spans beyond our specialty, he always, as his distinguished daughter Susan Schaeffer Macaulay once told me, saw the aerial picture of the whole forest in a way in which specialists, who knew their own twigs in detail, frequently, if not inevitably, failed to do.

In other words, Schaeffer saw the big picture of the modern condition. He understood that modern thinking was part of an intellectual system, an insight that many of his contemporary fellow evangelicals lacked. He could put the eternal truths of the gospel into language that could be understood by the first entirely post-Christian generations that followed the Second World War and, crucially, without in any way diluting the truths of the Christian faith in so doing. Like his contemporary and fellow giant of Reformed Evangelicalism Martyn Lloyd-Jones, he showed beyond doubt that the liberal claim that modern people would reject a supernatural gospel was entirely bogus—it was, in fact, *only* through the biblical message of redemption that mankind in the twentieth century had any hope at all.

Not only that, but I think that one of his most important books, *True Spirituality*, based upon Schaeffer's powerful experience of the Holy Spirit in the hayloft of L'Abri, and the idea it contains of *true truth* shows that one can legitimately call Schaeffer's ministry prophetic, a calling from God that would last for decades beyond his death in 1984.

We live now in a postmodern world, in which the whole concept of truth is denied, with all the repercussions that so negative a worldview has for us. There is a tendency to think that all this is new, and in many senses, certainly philosophically, that is probably correct. But, I would argue, God was giving Schaeffer the answers to all these issues way back in the 1950s, the biblical case for saying that there really is such a thing as absolute truth and that God in Christ is the only real truth and answer to the human predicament. This makes Francis Schaeffer, if anything, more relevant more than twenty years after his death than he was in his lifetime and a wonderful example of how God works through his faithful servants.

The work of L'Abri now continues in various places, not only in Switzerland, but in other parts of the world, and his books continue to reach out to new generations of Christians and those seeking the truth. His daughter Susan and her husband Ranald Macaulay in Cambridge, England are using one of that city's oldest church buildings, the medieval Round Church, to proclaim the timeless truths of the gospel to visitors from all over the world and to continue Schaeffer's great work of Christian apologetics to fortify believers in the twenty-first century.

C. S. Lewis

C. S. (Clive Staples) Lewis (1898–1963) is universally regarded as one of the greatest Christian writers and apologists of all time, as well as being one of the most distinguished literary professors of the twentieth century.

Lewis was born in Northern Ireland and lost his mother at an early age. His geographic distance from the heartlands of power and privilege and his tragic childhood made him an unlikely candidate for future fame, but also the brilliant writer that he turned out to be, since for him ease of living and youthful happiness were both unknown. He was also fortunate to survive the carnage of the First World War, in which millions of his contemporaries, both rich and poor, died needlessly in the trenches of Flanders and northern France. But despite all this his academic brilliance gained him a place at Oxford University, where he was to spend most of the rest of his life.

He began his early adulthood as an atheist. His Oxford contemporary, Vincent Lloyd-Jones, remembers being happily amazed to hear of his friend "Jack" Lewis's conversion in 1931. The fact that he had been an atheist, however, was to make him, like another former opponent of Christianity, the apostle Paul, into a far more powerful apologist once he had been converted, as he knew exactly what the opposition thought because he had once held to such ideas himself.

This special insight enabled him to write wonderful, still-read classics such as *Mere Christianity* and *The Screwtape Letters*, which were based upon radio broadcasts he made during the Second World War. These talks were to be costly, however. They outraged his snobbish colleagues at Oxford University, who thenceforth saw him as a popularizer despite the acknowledged brilliance of his literary lectures to university undergraduates. In fact, Lewis never became a full professor at Oxford—he stayed at the rank of a Fellow and Tutor at his college, Magdalen, and it was Cambridge University that gave him the higher honor, bestowing on him a chair in 1955 that he held for the rest of his life.

An expert on medieval and Renaissance literature, Lewis also had an instinctive understanding of the nature of allegory, a popular literary device. He was able to reemploy allegory in many of his apologetics books, but above all in his outstanding and deservedly well-loved novels—the science fiction books for adults and especially his brilliant Narnia stories for children, which still sell in the millions every year, now all the more so since the adaptation for cinema of the great classic *The Lion, the Witch and the Wardrobe*. These are not just fabulous stories for children that are not dated despite their Second World War setting. They are also some of the greatest Christian allegories ever written, with the truth of salvation shining through them for those who can find it.

Although Lewis is most highly regarded today among evangelicals—his papers and even the wardrobe itself are at Wheaton College in Wheaton, Illinois—he would always insist that he was a High Church member of the Church of England. This was a source of sorrow to evangelical pupils of his at Oxford, such as my mother, then Elizabeth Lloyd-Jones, Vincent's niece, but they all admired him deeply nonetheless and were thankful to God for all he did. But that in no way diminished the power of his written and radio ministry and the considerable help he has been to Christians ever since.

When it comes to allegory and a direct Christian message in fiction, Lewis was more overt than his academically more successful colleague, J.R.R. Tolkien, a fellow literature professor at Oxford and a devout Roman Catholic. Tolkien and Lewis were part of a Christian literary group, the Inklings, and each member was able to help the others in many useful ways. But Tolkien, while active in his faith, did not write books of apologetics, and he also, to the end of his life in 1973, always strongly denied that there was any element of allegory in his epic works such as The Lord of the Rings. This does not make them any less powerful or enjoyable, and millions of Christians have with good cause enjoyed reading them, but they lack that extra spiritual dimension that makes the Narnia stories so resonant for a Christian audience.

As with all the greatest writers and apologists, the work of C. S. Lewis is timeless and can be enjoyed as much by twenty-first-century audiences as by those who first read them decades ago.

Billy Graham

Billy Graham, born in 1918, was the best-known Christian preacher and evangelist of the twentieth century, a man with a worldwide reputation not only within Christian circles but well beyond them. As I wrote this book, for example, he received a profile in *Newsweek* magazine, several pages long, an accolade granted to few Christian leaders in these secular times.

William Franklin Graham was born in the American South and came from an underprivileged background. But he was educated, including at Wheaton College in Illinois, and was soon involved in God's calling for his life, a ministry of evangelism.

When I wrote about Billy Graham back in the 1980s, commentators emphasized to me that even though Graham was world-famous, he had never lost touch with his humble origins. As an *Orlando Sentinel* reporter put it, Billy Graham has "stayed folks." He still lives in an ordinary house in North Carolina, and from the beginning he insisted on a normal salary from the organization that he founded, the Billy Graham Evangelistic Association. This biblical lifestyle has never altered and meant that decades later, when several other evangelists and television preachers were mired in the dirt, Graham stayed pristine and fully compatible with a Scripture-based life as well as message. This in itself has been a powerful part of his witness—he has never been corrupted by fame and influence but has remained what he always set out to be, a faithful preacher of the message of salvation.

His fame on a national scale began in 1949 when a crusade—a word then without the unfortunate connotation it has developed in recent years—in San Francisco gained the attention of press mogul William Randolph Hearst. In 1954 Graham led a crusade in London, one that not only made him distinguished internationally but that can claim to have had lasting good effects on British Evangelicalism.

He then embarked on missions in countries where the gospel was not so easily preached. In India the missions were a considerable success. He also preached in the Soviet Union, where his willingness to cut deals with the Communist authorities in order to be able to preach made some Christians concerned. Many evangelicals, such as Martyn Lloyd-Jones in Britain, had always been worried by Graham's desire to have liberal as well as evangelical clergy on his crusade platforms. While Graham's motives have always been above reproach, other evangelists, such as Luis Palau, have enjoyed similar blessing on their missions without feeling the need to be quite so broad in choosing with whom they collaborate. On this issue readers can decide for themselves.

Graham has also been a facilitator, training evangelists from poor countries and bringing together evangelicals from all over the world in great gatherings such as those in Berlin in 1964 and, more notable, in Lausanne in 1974 (with Francis Schaeffer speaking at the latter). Here he has been an evangelical elder statesman along the lines of his British contemporary, the leading British Christian John Stott, whose work at Lausanne helped mark the public recognition of the growth of Evangelicalism in the Third World, (or Global South, as some prefer to call it). Graham's prestige and finance-raising credibility and Stott's commitment to biblical theology have had a lasting effect on worldwide Evangelicalism since that date, and it could be that this will prove just as important a part of Graham's enduring legacy as his more well-known crusades.

When abroad, it is also important to say that part of Graham's success—if one can call it that—has been his cultural sensitivity. While he is a famous American, he has always endeavored to preach in other countries simply as a fellow Christian, without imposing American methodology in nations where that might be deemed inappropriate by local evangelicals.

In the USA Graham has been an unofficial chaplain to many a U.S. President. After the Watergate debacle, when his closeness to Nixon got him in trouble by association, Graham has been understandably cautious and has eschewed all attempts to persuade him to play a political role. He also played a part in the conversion of President George W. Bush, one of America's few evangelical Presidents, although now, with Graham being much older and in poor health, his active participation in American Evangelicalism has naturally diminished.

Often forgotten is his resolute stand against racism as early as the 1950s when he, a southerner, insisted on fully racially integrated crusades, even in the South, something for which he deserves more credit than he has perhaps been given.

Martyn Lloyd-Jones

Dr. D. Martyn Lloyd-Jones (1899–1981), known familiarly to millions of evangelicals over the decades simply as "the Doctor," has been called the greatest expository preacher of the twentieth century.

(As his biographer, and maternal grandson, I have to declare a personal interest! Thankfully so many agree with the view I have just expressed that I am quite safe in expressing it here.)

He is best known, not just in Britain and the USA but also globally, for two major ministries.

The first is as pastor of Westminster Chapel in London from 1938 to 1968. His sermons were transcribed and have been turned into books that have been read worldwide by millions, thanks to publishers such as Crossway Books, and have been read even more since his death than in his lifetime.

The second was the pivotal role he played in the establishment after World War II of the International Fellowship of Evangelical Students (IFES), of which he was the founding chairman and later president and of which his daughter Elizabeth is a vice president today. Here his legacy also continues since IFES has stayed faithful to its biblical and evangelical roots and is now operating in more countries than ever before.

Martyn Lloyd-Jones was born into an economically poor but intellectually rich background, his father being a highly literate Welsh milkman. All three Lloyd-Jones boys were exceptionally gifted—one, Harold, died in the terrible influenza epidemic after World War II, and another, Vincent, an Oxford contemporary of C. S. Lewis, became a High Court Judge. Martyn became a medical student at an unusually early age and studied at one of Europe's oldest and top medical schools, St Bartholemew's in London. Here he gained his M.D. and was the star pupil of the king's physician, Lord Horder.

But Lloyd-Jones realized that God was in fact calling him into evangelistic and pastoral ministry in one of the poorest parts of South Wales, in Aberavon. His medical training had not been wasted though. He always maintained that his method of thinking and thus also of preaching in an expository way was profoundly influenced by learning to be a doctor. He described preaching as "logic on fire" or "theology coming through a man who is on fire," combining, as he would put it, the logic of Calvin with the fire of Methodism, not unlike his favorite American preacher, the great Jonathan Edwards, to whom he was so similar. His training in psychology was also helpful pastorally and led to one of his most appreciated works—*Spiritual Depression: Its Causes and Cure*.

After Wales he moved to Westminster Chapel, where his ministry became internationally famous, with people from all over the world in the congregation. Here he preached series that have sold in the millions—on Romans, Ephesians, John, Acts, and, if one includes his early Friday night lectures, great Christian doctrines. Many of these are still in print, notably with Crossway Books, a publisher regarded with deep affection by many in his family.

What is fascinating about the sermons is that they remain as fresh and relevant decades after they were first delivered. This is no coincidence. The Doctor's preaching was not designed to be trendy but timeless since he was expounding the eternally true and relevant Word of God. That is why he preached through a biblical book rather than topically and why as a result each sermon has a lasting quality that renders it readable today. This has resulted in his works being translated into many languages, since Koreans, for example, can grasp the message as easily as Britons or Americans.

Being Welsh enabled him to understand how many colonial subject nations felt, and this, along with his firm belief in the authority of Scripture, made a considerable difference to the way in which, for example, IFES was run. That movement believed in indigenous rather than Western-led leadership from the start, and in the case of IFES this was a principle of the organization long before much older Western-founded missionary societies realized the same thing should apply to them.

Martyn Lloyd-Jones was, along with figures such as Schaeffer, Graham, Stott, Packer, Henry, and others, one of the leaders of post-war renascent Evangelicalism, making sure that it was Scripture-grounded and faithful to the eternal message of salvation through Christ on the cross.

Like Schaeffer and Packer, he was also thoroughly Reformed in outlook, resurrecting Reformed theology for new generations of Christians. Here he was always careful to say that he was a "Bible Calvinist" rather than a "system Calvinist" since he believed what he did because of Scripture rather than because, say, Calvin or Edwards had said it, though he greatly admired such men and brought their work back to attention. His views on the work of the Holy Spirit or on the nature of the church did not bring unanimity among many of his followers since sincere evangelicals have disagreed for centuries on issues such as spiritual gifts or church structure. But everyone recognized that his opinions came from how he interpreted the Bible and what he honestly believed it had to say.

While it is over a quarter of a century since Dr. Lloyd-Jones's death, the work he began continues with his books, sermon audio ministry (now on CD-ROM and MP3), and a legacy as powerful now as ever.

Conclusion: Where Next?

In the original version of this book I quoted many statistics outlining the phenomenal growth of evangelical Christianity in the developing world and in more advanced but hitherto pagan nations such as China, India, and Korea. Statistics are, as people have pointed out to me since, perhaps misleading. This is possibly the case, though there might still be cause for rejoicing, since the overall pattern of millions of people in the Global South (the Third World) turning to Christian faith is true, even if completely accurate statistics are hard to come by.

For instance, the notion that there might be at least seventy-five million Christians in China could in fact be a wild underestimate—in subsequent years I have heard far higher figures quoted than that. But because the majority of evangelical Christians there are usually members of unregistered and thus illegal churches, it is impossible to tell with any real degree of accuracy. What we can tell for certain is that a church that was tiny and persecuted when the Protestant missionaries were expelled in the Reluctant Exodus of 1951 is now thriving and prospering as never before despite ongoing persecution. All the attempts of Mao Zedong and the violence of the Cultural Revolution, in which millions of innocent Chinese died, have in fact massively increased the numbers of Christians in China rather than wiping them out.

Likewise, it is possible that within this century Korea might become a majority Christian nation. Similarly if current growth trends continue, some of the countries of Latin America will be majority Protestant.

Here one needs to be careful. How would we as evangelicals classify some of the doctrinally stranger health and wealth prosperity teaching movements in, say, Brazil? If statistics include them, I would be worried.

Back in 1989 some very eminent secular publications, in making their prognostications for later 1989 through 1990, all missed one of the most significant historical events of the twentieth century—the downfall, without war or mass bloodshed, of the Communist regimes in central and eastern Europe. Almost none of the experts, however eminent, predicted it; yet the demise of Communism without World War III completely changed everything.

Prognostication is therefore a very hazardous thing to attempt.

Until the end of the carnage of the Cultural Revolution, it was almost impossible to find out what was happening in China, for instance. Yet the reality, however astonishing it might seem, is that despite all the persecution, torture, mass killings, and general chaos, millions of Chinese were becoming Christians. This is a wonderful thing and a mighty work of God. Yet humanly speaking who would ever have predicted it?

Likewise, the Church of England globally—the Anglican Communion—has been completely transformed by the tremendous wave of conversions to evangelical Christian faith in areas such as West Africa, southeast Asia, and Latin America. In this instance the growth has been so remarkable that even secular sociologists in Western universities have been forced to notice it and ponder its ramifications. The fight within the Anglican Communion for a return to biblical doctrines and moral standards is led from places such as Nigeria (where there are seventeen times as many Anglicans as practicing Christians in the whole of England) and Argentina against the rampant Liberalism of Episcopalians in the USA and Canada. This too is a new, exciting, and yet possibly unpredicted development.

Certainly the optimism of my 1998 edition has not been misplaced. We evangelicals can be assured that God is at work in our world today and that the gospel can never be defeated by even the most vicious human enemies. As I suggested in another book (on Islam), if the whole massive edifice of Communism could collapse like a house of cards between 1989 and 1991, when the Soviet Union itself imploded, then who knows what God might do next! In the twenty-first century the solid bloc of Islam—from Morocco in the west to Indonesia in the east—seems, from most rational vantage points, to be insuperable. Yet so too once did the Communist Empire, and while China remains at least nominally Communist, the church there is thriving.

Why, therefore, should we view the Islamic world as impervious? Once pagan Nigeria is sending missionaries to now godless Britain. Do we believe in the power of God completely to thwart His enemies and confound their purposes? Egypt, Iraq, Syria, Tunisia—all these were once majority Christian regions, the original lands of the Christian faith. Why should they not be so again? Biblically, there is no reason why the frontiers of Islam should not be pushed back—not by armies as in the past, but by the power of God's Word and His message of salvation. If, like me, you are a Reformed evangelical, surely there should be even more grounds for optimism since God can turn even the hardest hearts to faith and repentance in Jesus Christ.

Never before in history has so much of the globe heard the message of Christian truth. We could, indeed, be on the edge of truly exciting times.

Index

218